OLD FAVORITES
In Miniature

by Tina M. Gravatt

DEDICATION

This book is dedicated to my students

who have helped to keep me inspired and challenged

through their many questions, their helpful suggestions,

and the many lovely quilts that they have made.

Other books by Tina M. Gravatt:
Heirloom Miniatures (AQS)

Gravatt, Tina M.
    Old favorites in miniature / by Tina M. Gravatt.
        p.   cm.
    Includes bibliographical references.
    ISBN 0-89145-808-5 : $15.95
        1. Quilting--Patterns. 2. Patchwork--Patterns.   3. Miniature
quilts.   I. Title.
TT835.G732   1993   93-15891
746.9'7'0228--dc20   CIP

Additional copies of this book may be ordered from:

American Quilter's Society
P.O. Box 3290
Paducah, KY 42002-3290
@15.95. Add $1.00 for postage and handling.

Copyright: Tina M. Gravatt, 1993

FOREWORD

Lilliput and that strange land *Through the Looking Glass* are not just for the young. *The Borrowers* is the kind of book that adults read to children, but often for their own enjoyment. Very few grown-ups would turn down a chance to spend a day in a world of doll-size furniture and dainty little linens. There is something soothing about folding the quilts and blankets and smoothing out the sheets for a doll bed, as opposed to struggling with overwhelming king-size coverings.

Doll quilts have been made by little girls and their mothers and grandmothers for a century or so. Recently, they became collector's items, catching the imagination of well-known collector-writers like Thomas. K. Woodard and Blanche Greenstein, authors of *Crib Quilts and Other Small Wonders*, who point out that many doll quilts were simply cut-downs from larger outworn household quilts, but the most valued ones were made to scale, looking for all the world like the bed quilts from which they were derived.

The first time I encountered Tina Gravatt's growing collection of quilts and doll beds at a large show, I could hardly believe the perfection of the work. My eyes were deceived by the exact scale of quilts to beds so that I felt that I was looking at a very fine collection of antiques, quilts all perfectly matched to beds in size and style. There were beautifully worked *broderie perse* quilts for the grand four-poster beds and scrappy country quilts for crudely crafted farm-house pieces. Later I saw them photographed in appropriate room sets and the illusion was even more complete.

For the many people who have kept precious doll beds from their childhood or bought one or two at auction "because they were just too good to pass up," this book should be all the inspiration needed to clothe that furniture and put it on display. There are styles for every era and every type of furniture, some easy enough for beginners and some a challenge to the best of quilters. For anyone who has sewed or made large quilts, this will be the answer to the problem of saving tiny scraps "too small to save." Trading scraps with other quilters will undoubtedly bring in any extra pieces needed.

The delight in actually completing a quilt and looking at it on a bed is a feeling well-known to the initiated and hard to describe to the outsider. Even though tiny quilts can have a high degree of difficulty, they can still be finished in less time than full-size quilts – and bring the same feeling of euphoria!

— Carter Houck

TABLE OF CONTENTS

INTRODUCTION

I began collecting doll beds by mistake! I wanted to display the miniature quilts I was making in a way that would make them look like what they are – scaled-down versions of full-size bed quilts. I went to a local toy store and bought a simple white metal doll bed. I made mattresses, pillows, pillowcases, sheets, a blanket, and a dust ruffle, and then placed my quilt on top. The effect was perfect; seen through a camera lens, the quilt and bed looked as if they were adult size.

The effect of a doll bed on a miniature quilt is much the same as the effect of a picture frame on a painting. It causes the viewer to see different things and to focus on different features than if the quilt or painting were left plain. I began to notice that just as the bed was having an effect on the quilt, the quilt was having an effect on the bed. Different features, such as head and footboard details, were enhanced or diminished depending upon the styling and color of the quilt.

In the beginning, I bought my beds at large toy supermarkets; later I began to check out local thrift shops, garage sales, and flea markets. Now I'm an aficionado of antique shops and malls. The price of a bed isn't the most important criterion for selection. What is important is that the bed has a large enough top surface to allow for the proper display of the quilt's pattern, and enough depth on the sides to allow the quilt to drape successfully and show off its borders. Each bed and each quilt brings its own character to the other, creating a very special effect.

For me, collecting the beds has become as interesting a project as making the miniature quilts that will grace them. The beds come in all sizes, shapes, colors, and materials – wood, twigs, cast iron, plastic, wire, paper, etc. They represent all time periods, the oldest known toy bed being one found in a Greek child's tomb from the third century A.D. Catherine Beecher (Harriet Beecher Stowe's sister) recommended the use of doll beds as instructional items in her book, *Treatise on Domestic Economy for Use of Young Ladies at Home and at School,* published in 1841. She wrote, "When a little girl begins to sew, her mother can promise her a small bed (mattress) and pillow, as soon as she has sewed a patch quilt for them; and then a bedstead (bed), as soon as she has sewed the sheets and cases for the pillows…."

If you should become involved in doll bed collecting, the oldest advice is still the best. Buy only that which you like. You are the one who has to look at it, and hopefully, you are the one who will dress it and provide it with a quilt of such perfect styling and scale that when it is seen in a photo, no one will know it is not the full-size bed in which you sleep each night!

First, and foremost, I am a quilter and lover of quilts. I would love to own all the antique quilts I see. I would love to make one of each and every pattern available to quilters today. Realistically, no one can accomplish such an enormous task. However, by creating small quilts, it is possible to produce and enjoy a broad spectrum of quilts. You, the quiltmaker, can experiment with all types of different styles and techniques. Miniature quilts can be hand pieced, machine pieced, quick pieced using any of the new rotary cutter and strip piecing techniques; they can be appliquéd, whole cloth, marbleized, sun-printed, embellished, embroidered – whatever you want!

In my books I always try to include patterns for quilts that you may not have thought about making in miniature. This book includes a 25-block Baltimore Album style quilt, a Union quilt with shields, a Victorian silk biscuit quilt with lace edging, a 1930's Water Lilies appliqué, an Umbrella quilt done as a charm quilt, and a sun-print snowflake pattern quilt. For this second book I have rewritten the General Instructions and added information for all areas of miniature quiltmaking. There is a Resource List which will help you find the supplies and materials needed to make planning and constructing miniature quilts more pleasurable. I hope you will enjoy this book as much as you did the first one.

Part I

The Quilts & Their Histories

The quilts selected for this book cover 200 years of American quilting history. They include one quilt in a late eighteenth-century style, nine quilts from the nineteenth century, four from the first half of the twentieth century, one contemporary, and four of Pennsylvania German heritage.

When making quilts today, it is often impossible to *exactly* match the colors of old quilts. Instead, I strive to capture the essence of the quilts of the past. Sometimes I use modern fabrics which are reprints of old ones, and sometimes I include old fabric. I look for similarity in mood, i.e., texture, styling, etc. Occasionally, I update an old pattern with contemporary colors. My goal is to strive for a miniature quilt with color balance, proper scale, and good graphics, and one which is pleasing whether displayed on a doll bed or as a wall decoration.

WHOLE CLOTH (Plate I)

Variously known as calimanco, linsey-woolsey, glazed wool or whole cloth quilts, these spreads or counterpanes were part of the fashionable necessities of the well-dressed bed of the late eighteenth century in America. The motifs on these quilts were inspired by design books, embroideries, and fancy chintz goods from India and the Dutch East Indies. Some of these quilts had a soft gloss finish achieved either by rubbing the fabric with a stone or by applying egg white and water to the fabric before constructing the quilt.

In order to duplicate this look using the fabrics available today, I chose a deep red polished cotton for the front or top of the quilt, and an unglazed yellow cotton for the backing. This color combination closely resembles a 1775 quilt with deep watermelon pink on the front and bright yellow on the reverse.

My quilt was designed for an eighteenth century "toy" cradle. (The word "toy" did not always refer to a

child's plaything; it was also used to denote an object made for adult amusement or pleasure.) Made from mahogany, the cradle has two round ivory knobs on each side and a curved hood. It is long, narrow, and deep. I began by making a false bottom for the cradle, and then made two mattresses, a pillow, and linens. The quilt was designed to either drape over the top of the cradle or tuck inside around the mattresses and linens. I used a medallion format, common in late eighteenth- and early nineteenth-century quilts. The center motif combines four stems with feathered curves around a circle. It is surrounded by a feathered border with hearts, which is surrounded by another border containing a vine, leaves, two more hearts, and paisley shapes in each of the four corners. The patterns are somewhat Jacobean in origin, much like the crewelwork motifs that were popular on late eighteenth-century bed hanging embroideries. Many of the old quilts were quilted with matching thread, and I have done the same in this quilt.

SUNBURST (Plate II)

At first glance, this miniature quilt may appear to be just one block from a full-size quilt used on its own as a small quilt. However, there are full-size quilts from the late eighteenth and early nineteenth centuries with a one-block pattern for the overall motif. These patterns, reduced in size, continued to be used on quilts throughout the nineteenth century, in the more familiar block-repeat format.

My Sunburst quilt was inspired by an 1810 Ohio quilt made from one large compass-like block. The original quilt was somewhat primitive and lacked borders. I tried to make my quilt more sophisticated by carefully repeating a flower pattern in all the outer points and adding a striped border. There is stipple quilting in the center circle around the flowers and geometric shapes.

The rays are quilted ¼" inside the seam lines and the area around the sunburst is quilted in ¼" concentric rows, reinforcing the circular motion of the sunburst itself. The colors are not totally faithful to the early nineteenth century, but do convey the mood of the time.

BETHLEHEM STAR (Plate III)

Star quilts may well head the list in historical popularity. They come in all sizes and shapes. Some of the large-format stars, variously known as Star of Bethlehem, Star of the East, Rising Sun, Blazing Star or Lone Star, could reach dimensions in excess of 100" x 100" square! Cutting out hundreds – even thousands – of diamonds and then sewing them together into a large overall design that remained on grain and square was only for expert quiltmakers, whose workmanship can still be seen today in examples from the first half of the nineteenth century. These quilts were "best spreads" or counterpanes (the outermost coverings used on beds, primarily for decoration rather than warmth).

Today we no longer need to cut out each individual diamond; instead we can sew strips together, cutting them on a 45-degree angle to quick piece this style of quilt. I used this technique to construct my miniature. I still wanted it to have the "feel" of the old ones. Therefore, I chose printed cottons that would emulate beautiful chintzes, early calicoes, and imported English and French goods. I used a large brown and green paisley print, a small all-over white and yellow calico, a small all-over blue and white paisley, an almost Oriental type white and blue geometric design, and an 1880's blue, white, and black swirl fabric. When cut apart for the star, their lack of evenness and the fact that only a small area of each pattern shows, add to their old look.

Since these quilts have eight points, or legs, they produce large empty squares in the corners and triangles between the points. These areas were filled with appliqué images, *broderie perse* designs, (small stars as in mine), or left plain to show off the quiltmakers' quilting patterns and skills.

I chose to add a double border to complete my quilt and it is quilted "in the ditch" around all the dia-

monds in the large and small stars. In addition, there are small quilted stars in the corners and triangles.

INDIGO BLUE & WHITE (Plate IV)

Stylized tree motifs were used on quilts in the Southern and Mid-Atlantic states from the 1830's through the mid-1860's. Sometimes, they would appear in one block of an album quilt, while other times they would make up the border on an Irish Chain or other patchwork-style quilt. Some quilt historians call them Palm Trees while others label them as Weeping Willows. Whatever the original quiltmaker's intent may have been, these quilts have a folk-art look that is highly prized today.

Several years ago I purchased an old doll bed, and like most of the beds I acquire, it came without any information about its origin or age. My only clues were the hand-painted wood grain finish and its unique headboard that resembled the tree motifs on the old quilts. I believed my bed to be of a similar period and decided that I would use its trees for my quilt's design.

I chose two different indigo-like blue and white prints for my trees and Sawtooth borders. Two different size trees are repeated in parallel rows in the body of the quilt, and still more trees surround three of the sides in the border; but no trees were applied to the top border. The decision to leave one side plain came from seeing some nineteenth-century quilts on which this was done. Usually the plain edge was on the side next to the wall, where the work wouldn't show, or at the top of the quilt where the border could be tucked out of sight behind the pillow.

The trees and Sawtooth borders were outline quilted, and the top border treated as if it had been constructed the same as the sides. Birds and circles were added over the small trees in the center.

DELECTABLE MOUNTAINS (Plate V)

The old quilt pattern Delectable Mountains took its name from John Bunyan's book *Pilgrim's Progress*, published in England in 1678. In this allegory of man's search for heaven, near the end of the journey, the Pilgrim reaches the Delectable Mountains, covered in bounty (orchards, vineyards, and gardens)[1] with a view of the Celestial City (heaven). All this may sound a bit esoteric for pioneers in America in the nineteenth century, but in fact, in many homes John Bunyan's story was often the only book other than the Bible.

It is tempting to romanticize the pioneer times in America and relate their trials to those of the "Pilgrim," thereby explaining the popularity of this quilt pattern. Whatever the real reasons may have been, it was a quilt that required accurate piecing and math skills. I can make this last statement with confidence, as I have spent many days working out the math on the two Delectable Mountains quilts I have made.

My red, green, and gold quilt has the mountains arranged in horizontal rows across the quilt top. In the large triangles between the mountains I have quilted a rosette pattern. It is a strikingly graphic quilt that looks good both on a doll bed and on the wall.

BALTIMORE ALBUM STYLE QUILT (Plate VI)

A very popular type of appliqué quilt was the Album style. The most impressive and beautiful of these were made in Baltimore, Maryland, between the early years of the 1840's and the second half of the 1850's. The complexity of the motifs and the high quality of workmanship made these quilts surpass other Album styles. They were large, sometimes reaching dimensions of almost 10' x 12'! The blocks were from 15" to 34" square. To reproduce such a quilt in miniature is a challenge best left to the skilled needleworker.

I began by studying old Album quilt blocks. I found the most popular designs were wreaths, vases and baskets of flowers and fruits; religious and organizational symbols; wildlife; and local monuments and structures. As I discuss later in the General Instructions, artistic license is often necessary when reducing a full-size quilt block into miniature. In this quilt I used embroidery to create stems, vines, leaves, flower details, a basket, and a peacock-like bird. I also used yo-yos to create many of the flowers and some of the stuffed details. However, I did not use any Baltimore city buildings or monuments in my quilt; because my Album quilt was being made in Philadelphia, I chose Independence Hall and the Declaration of Independence.

I completed the quilt top by bordering it in the classic mid-nineteenth century style of swags and tassels.

Each block motif is quilted close to the appliqué seams and embroidery stitches, so that the eye is not confused by the scale of the quilting stitches versus the embroidery stitches.

When I made this quilt, I had only just begun collecting doll beds and owned only five. It wasn't until three years after this quilt had been completed that the perfect bed for it came into my possession. It is a circa 1840-60 spool bed with pine tree finials on each of the four posts. Although the bed has a somewhat simple look to it, all the turnings are handmade and quite well done. When the Album quilt is placed on this simple bed, it becomes more sophisticated and its dark coloring shows off the light background of the quilt.

UNION QUILT (Plate VII)

National events, political campaigns, and armed conflicts all had strong influences on women's lives and their needlework. It is estimated that through the Soldiers' Aid Societies, 250,000 quilts were donated to the troops during the Civil War.

Without access to the ballot box, women in both the North and the South expressed their patriotism by means of the needle. There is a patchwork pillow made from homespun cotton with a poem about the skills and hardships of Southern women.[2] There are Northern quilts with inked quotations of nationalism and personal feeling, i.e.: "While our fingers guide the needle, Our hearts are intense [in tents]."[3]

Since the beginning of our nation, women have created quilts using red, white, and blue; symbols, such as stars, stripes, shields, and eagles; and patchwork patterns such as 54-40 or Fight and Whigs' Defeat to demonstrate their patriotism.[4]

For my quilt, I chose a shield motif and used red, white, and blue star prints. For the lower section of the shields I chose pinstripes and mattress-ticking fabrics. These proved most effective, as they were in scale with the small shields and their stripe widths varied, which helped keep the simple motif from becoming boring. The quilting is done around each shield, and the overall effect is quite dramatic and very patriotic for such a small quilt.

BISCUIT QUILT (Plate VIII)

At first glance, the visual effect of a biscuit quilt suggests a difficult construction technique: all those little square puffs of silk, each pleated on all sides. However, the puffs are surprisingly easy to make – they are two different size squares of fabric which are sewn together and stuffed.

In my research I have found two silk biscuit quilts. One was made in 1874 in Nova Scotia, as a present for the quiltmaker's only son. This quilt was made from Victorian dress silks, including brocades and embossed fabrics. The other was a child's quilt or a lap robe which was exhibited at the Milwaukee Public Museum in 1985-86. These novelty quilts were edged with either ruffling or lace.

I chose the lace treatment for my miniature. This quilt provides the perfect opportunity to use old hand- or machine-made lace you may have inherited or just couldn't resist buying at a yard sale. The "biscuits" in my quilt are made from the silk used for men's ties. I acquired my fabric in England while on a teaching trip there, but you can use old ties purchased from thrift shops, being sure to launder them first!

ELONGATED HEXAGON (Plate IX)

When we think of the late 1800's, we think of crazy quilts, novelty quilts, and charm quilts. As quilt historian Cuesta Benberry explained in an article on the subject, "Charm quilt is an umbrella term referring to the composition of the quilt rather than to a specific pattern."[5]

A traditional charm quilt is one in which no two patches are alike. The pieces are cut from just one template and set side-by-side without sashings. More often than not, the "charm" or allure of these quilts was in the collecting and trading done to obtain the fabric necessary to make the quilt. Frequently, the traditional charm quilt contained 999 different pieces. Many years were needed to collect so much different fabric, and more than one generation could be involved in the saving of scraps for such a quilt. Not every charm quilt from the 1870's and 1880's was composed of such a large number of fabrics. There are quilts that used large patches and contain only a few hundred pieces.

The inspiration for my miniature charm quilt came from an 1875 quilt pictured in the November-December 1990 issue of *Lady's Circle Patchwork Quilts*. That charm quilt was made from elongated hexagons arranged in a Trip around the World setting. The colors were browns, yellows, and beige with a little red, dark blue, black, and gray added for interest.

I wanted to duplicate the old quilt as closely as possible; I sorted through my fabric stacks and cut a square from each of the appropriate colors. Since this quilt was to be my traveling companion to Europe, I prepared my templates – paper pieces – and fabrics, and placed them in little plastic bags.

As I traveled and taught, I begged still more fabric from students and hostesses, but when I returned home five weeks later, I was still in need of a few more prints to complete the quilt. My quilting group came to the rescue, and within ten days, the top was complete. There are 351 different fabrics in my miniature. The hexagons are appliquéd to a background fabric which forms the borders and there is no quilting; instead, the quilt is tied with embroidery floss on the reverse. The use of novelty prints and patriotic symbols gives this quilt interesting details like those contained in the original.

TRIP AROUND THE WORLD (Plate X)

Traveling along U.S. Route 30 in Lancaster County, Pennsylvania, the tourist is struck by the dramatic graphic effect achieved by a patchwork quilt known as Trip around the World. These quilts seem to be everywhere – on porch railings, draped over shrubbery, and on clotheslines. This being Lancaster County, you might expect all these quilts to be made from solid colors and to display a strong Amish origin, but most are made from print fabrics of virtually all colors of the rainbow.

Trip around the World is an old patchwork design which seems to date to around the turn-of-the-century and was made by Amish, Mennonites, Pennsylvania Germans, and their "English" (as anyone non-German is called) neighbors. The pattern is also known as Sunshine and Shadow and can even be made as a charm quilt using one color in all different prints for each diamond row.

I chose blues, burgundy, pink, beige, and gray for my quilt. These colors create a soft appearance without detracting from the quilt's graphic impact. It is quilted in each color row on the diagonal through the middle of the block, further enhancing the "trip" effect. The wide border provides a traditional finish.

WATER LILIES (Plate XI)

The state quilt research projects have been exceedingly helpful to those of us who count ourselves as quilt historians as well as those of us who just like quilts.

These projects provide inspiration for design, color, format, border ideas, etc. I rely on the project books for new ideas and they also rekindle interest in colors and patterns once thought to be *passé*.

While re-reading Jeanette Lasansky's *In the Heart of Pennsylvania, Nineteenth and Twentieth Century Quiltmaking Traditions*, I saw a photo of a Water Lilies quilt made in the 1930's. It was made from a Home Art Company quilt kit. The colors were simple but effective, and I felt the design would make a lovely miniature quilt.

After drafting out the pattern, photocopying it, and trying the idea out on a bed, it became evident that the photograph of the quilt had been accidentally inverted in the book. I knew this because there was a large area of open space at one end of the quilt indicating that it must have been planned as the "tuck in" under the pillow. By turning the quilt with the other end up, it made more sense and the pattern even looked more pleasing.

In looking at my quilt, the background "water" fabric may appear to be hand-dyed; it is not. It was printed to look that way. Since the background is unevenly dyed, it is a perfect fabric to represent water. The appliquéd leaves are "Nile green," a color popular in the 1930's, and each lily petal is sewn on separately. To complete the flower, there is a yellow yo-yo in the center. The quilting is done in a free-form pattern to emulate ripples in the water.

My search for just the right bed to fit this quilt was both long and difficult. The bed needed to look like a colonial revival style bed of the 1930's without actually being an eighteenth- or nineteenth-century doll bed. I found a circa 1950's rope-strung, four-poster bed with pineapple finials. The headboard was styled in a simple curve similar to the many eighteenth-century beds. The bed was perfect, except for the fact that its finish had been water stained, one of the side rails was missing, and it was over-priced! Even so, I bought it, stripped off the finish, had a friend make a new rail and re-glue all the loose joints, and I then refinished it. After much hard work, the quilt and bed were united.

GRANDMOTHER'S FLOWER GARDEN (Plate XII)

When I began making miniature quilts, I didn't like the traditional hexagon patterns. I made one for my first lecture series and thought I'd never have to make another. Now, five hexagon quilts later, I have discovered that, with their endless color and arrangement possibilities, hexagon quilts are very satisfying to design.

In 1935 Carrie A. Hall wrote in *The Romance of the Patchwork Quilt* about the popularity of the Grandmother's Flower Garden pattern and the quiltmaker's pride in the number of small hexagons necessary to finish such a quilt. I can't say that I would look forward to the thousands of half-inch hexagons necessary to make a full-size quilt, but I find the handwork required for a miniature very satisfying.

I wanted my quilt to have as classic a 1930's look as possible, so I went through my old fabric collection and tried to find suitable pieces. I found, instead, that many of the 1930's fabrics were printed on white backgrounds with large "bleed" areas between the printed designs. On the small hexagons needed for my quilt, too much background would mean that the edges would bleed into the garden "paths" and distort the shapes of the rosettes. My alternative was to use Liberty of London prints which had a 1930's look but didn't have the large "white" areas. I also used some American prints and combined 27 different fabrics to produce the rosette "flowers." I used muslin for the garden paths and set one light green hexagon between each rosette. I put a thin layer of batting inside this quilt, tied it on the front with embroidery floss, and kept the hexagon shape on the sides.

UMBRELLAS (Plate XIII)

Wherever I go, I look at quilts. So it was only natural that, at a quilt convention in Virginia, I would spend every minute that I wasn't teaching or lecturing at the vendors' mall! I discovered many lovely quilts, but to paraphrase an old cliché, "many were seen but few were chosen."

I found two quilts that I wanted to interpret in miniature, one of which I purchased. The other, an umbrella quilt, the owner let me photograph. I'd not seen the pattern before, although I have subsequently had several people tell me that they have seen such a quilt. The umbrella was made by cleverly using a part of the Double Wedding Ring pattern. The small solid area between the rings becomes the top of the umbrella, while the ring segments become the sides.

The original quilt was made from 1930's fabrics with a disproportionately wide sashing and even wider border. My interpretation used old and new fabrics with each umbrella wedge being different. The resulting quilt can be classified as a charm quilt because no one fabric is used twice. I added lavender sashings and borders and quilted around each umbrella and all block seams. There are elliptical quilting patterns in the borders and the sashings.

SCOTTIE DOGS (Plate XIV)

In the 1930's, with quilting a renewed art form, and patchwork patterns appearing weekly in local newspapers, few themes escaped quilters' notice. The election of Franklin Delano Roosevelt in 1932 brought hope to an economically depressed nation. "New Deal," NRA (National Recovery Act), TVA (Tennessee Valley Authority), and the President's enthusiastic and photogenic Scottie dog Fala (often seen with him on newsreels) all appeared on quilts. The Scotties were very popular on children's quilts and were interpreted both in patchwork and appliqué patterns. Many of the dogs were made from plaid fabrics; others were made from anything in the scrap bag.

My quilt is scrap-like but was planned so that there would be two dogs from each fabric, thereby balancing the quilt. The dogs were appliquéd to one large background piece and then quilted to make them appear as if assembled in blocks. A single border was added, but a different fabric was used for the binding to give the effect of a smaller border treatment.

SNOWFLAKES (Plate XV)

The many different books and kits available today cover a wide range of new techniques. Often, experimentation with these can be done in miniature. I decided to try a cyanotype print, a light-exposure, blueprint-like technique. Since I had had no experience in this area, to improve my chances of success, I purchased a kit with chemically impregnated muslin squares. I cut the squares down to 3½" and I made a cardboard snowflake for my image. Following the package instructions, I repeated this image on 20 blocks. The blocks were then set with ½" wide sashings and finished off with a 2" border.

The quilting was done around the snowflake shapes and all of the seam lines. I designed a Spinning Star pattern for the borders and bound the quilt with a narrow bias binding.

AMISH DIAMOND IN A SQUARE (Plate XVI)

The religious persecution suffered by the Quakers in England caused William Penn to determine that his colony in the New World would provide religious freedom to all who settled there. During the mid-to-late eighteenth century, many of the new settlers to Pennsylvania were of German origin. Some came from strict religious groups to whom religion was not just theoretical or intellectual dogma, but rather a part of everyday living. Accordingly, each day's work was treated with reverence and pride of workmanship.

Nowhere is this fact seen so clearly as in the Pennsylvania quilts of the Lancaster County Old Order Amish. These Amish quiltmakers use simple graphics and bold colors, often in strongly contrasting combinations. One of the most common quilt designs is the Diamond in the Square. It consists of a square set on point in the center of the quilt, surrounded by a narrow border with corner squares. This, in turn, is surrounded by large triangles, another narrow border, and, finally, a wide border with four corner squares.

It is the quilting that transforms these quilts into works of art. They are heavily quilted with many different patterns which create a bas-relief surface upon which light dances. My miniature has feathered vines, rosettes, concentric diamonds, pumpkin seeds, grid fillings in both ½" and ¼" rows, a double star in the center, and a feather wreath in each of the four corners.

JOSEPH'S COAT & ZIGZAG (Plates XVII & XVIII)

To me, these two quilts are as one because both were inspired by the strong Pennsylvania German influence in American quilts, an influence so strong as to cause quilt historian and curator Sandi Fox to write: "The distinctive quilts of the Pennsylvania Germans are among the most identifiable as have come from a particular region — in many ways they are the most surprising of colors, most joyful of design."[6]

I made these two quilts to fit a set of contemporary doll bunkbeds. The beds were painted avocado green, yellow, and blue. I wanted to repaint them white, but was encouraged by my family to meet the challenge of using them just as they had come from the toy store. Since I hate doing anything twice, I decided to make coordinating quilts instead of a matched pair. I looked at many old quilts for inspiration but finally settled on the bold graphics and bright colors of the Pennsylvania Germans because these quilts would "hold their own" on the beds. I used most of the same colors in both quilts, but created an overall effect of red for the Joseph's Coat and blue for the Zigzag. Therefore, they are bound in those colors and each bed's pillowcase matches the color of the quilt's binding.

THISTLE CRADLE QUILT (Plate XIX)

Fortunately, some of our quilt history has been saved and is being preserved at museums and historical societies throughout the country. One such institution is the Pennsylvania Farm Museum which illustrates the farming life of rural Pennsylvania. Among its many artifacts are some lovely quilts. Several of these caught the eye of Carter Houck and Myron Miller when they were developing their book *American Quilts and How to Make Them*.

I discovered the Thistle Crib Quilt pattern in their book. I needed a long, vertical image for a reproduction eighteenth-century hooded cradle. After studying the essence of the old quilt, I decided to keep certain design elements, and change others to suit my needs.

I used the large rosette flower shape from the center of the old quilt, then I changed the leaves into more of an oak-leaf shape and made trumpet-like images for the flowers. I kept the red, pink, and orange color scheme of many Pennsylvania German quilts, but in order to be sure the quilt would look old, I used antique fabrics for the flowers, leaves, stem, and Sawtooth border. The background fabric is a dark beige, almost a light brown, which was chosen to give an old "yellowed" appearance to the new quilt. The quilting follows the seam lines and appliqué shapes. The background is filled with a quilted diamond grid in double parallel rows 1" apart. The effect of a bright pink-and-green quilt against the walnut stain of the cradle is most effective.

FOOTNOTES

[1]Fox, Sandi. *19th Century American Patchwork Quilt*. The Seibu Museum of Art Catalogue, Japan 1983. Quotation from John Bunyan's *Pilgrim's Progress* "... the Delectable Mountains. "...and behold at a great distance he saw a most pleasant, Mountainous Country, Beautified with Woods, Vineyards, Fruits of all sorts, Flowers also, with Springs and Fountains, very delectable to behold...And when thou comest there, from thence, said they, thou mayest see to the gate of the Celestial City....".

[2]Ferrero, Pat, Elaine Hedges, Julie Silber. *Hearts and Hands, the Influence of Women and Quilts on American Society*. Quilt Digest Press, San Francisco, CA, 1987, page 79. Pillow made from homespun cottons with embroidery in a crazy patch fashion. Embroidered on the cushion are the words: "'Hooray! for the home spun dresses we southern ladies wore in time of the war. Ev'ry piece here, Sad memories it brings back to me, For our hearts was weary and restless, And our life was full of care, The burden laid upon us seemed greater than we could bear.' Mary Prince, 1910, age 70 years."

[3]*Ibid*: page 75. Quilt with stars and shield, 1864, 71" X 81", pieced and appliquéd cottons, with ink work and embroidery, Portland, ME.

[4]Khin, Yvonne M. *The Collector's Dictionary of Quilt Names and Patterns*, Acropolis Books, Ltd., Washington, D.C., 1980, p. 138, "54-40 or FIGHT", the popular slogan in the 1830's-40's, during the boundary dispute between the United States and Great Britain over the Oregon Territory. Page 388, Whig's Defeat, a pattern designed at the time of the election of 1844 when the Whig presidential candidate, Henry Clay, was defeated by the Democrat, James K. Polk.

[5]Benberry, Cuesta. "Charm Quilts." *Quilter's Newsletter Magazine*, March 1980, p.14.

[6]Fox, Sandi; curator. *19th-Century American Patchwork Quilt*. The Seibu Museum of Art Catalogue, Japan, 1983. Writing about Plate 28.

Old Favorites
in Miniature

COLOR PLATE SECTION

Plate I. *WHOLE CLOTH, 14½" x 19½", © 1990.*

Plate II. *SUNBURST, 19½" x 19½", © 1986.*

Plate III. *BETHLEHEM STAR, 24" x 24", © 1989.*

Plate IV. *INDIGO BLUE & WHITE, 20" x 23½,"*
© 1990.

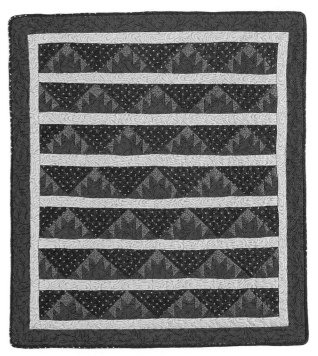

Plate V. *DELECTABLE MOUNTAINS, 16" x 18", © 1990.*

Plate VI. *BALTIMORE ALBUM STYLE QUILT,*
24" x 24", © 1986.

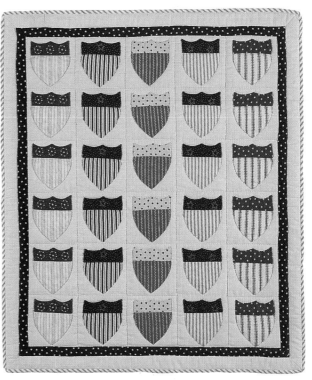

Plate VII. *UNION QUILT, 17¾" x 20½", © 1990.*

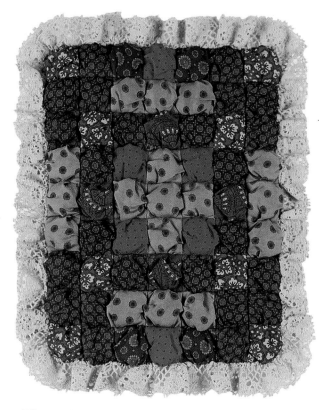

Plate VIII. *BISCUIT QUILT, 9½" x 11½", © 1990.*

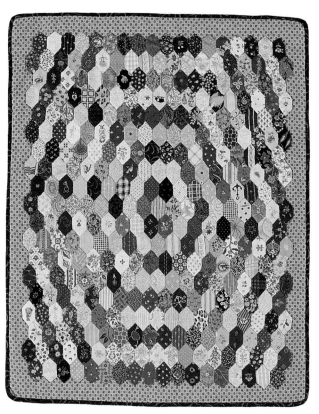

Plate IX. *ELONGATED HEXAGON CHARM, 15" x 19", © 1990.*

Plate X. *TRIP AROUND THE WORLD, 21" x 21", © 1986.*

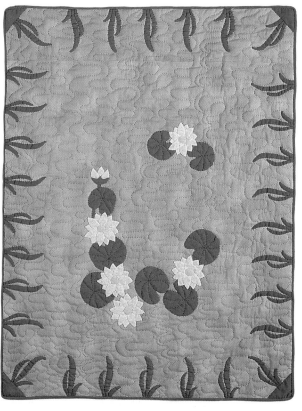

Plate XI. *WATER LILIES, 20½" x 26½", © 1991.*

Plate XII. *GRANDMOTHER'S FLOWER GARDEN, 21⅞" x 25½", © 1991.*

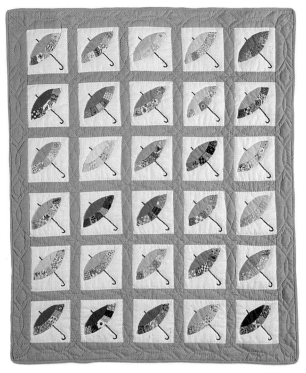

Plate XIII. *UMBRELLAS, 19½" x 23¼", © 1991.*

Plate XIV. *SCOTTIE DOGS, 15¾" x 21½", © 1990.*

Plate XV. *SNOWFLAKES, 19" x 22½", © 1990.*

17

Plate XVI. AMISH *DIAMOND IN A SQUARE, 20½" x 20½", © 1986.*

Plate XVII. *JOSEPH'S COAT, 18½" x 23", © 1987.*

Plate XVIII. *ZIGZAG, 18½" x 22½", © 1987.*

Plate XIX. *THISTLE CRADLE QUILT, 17½" x 23½", © 1990.*

Part II

Making the Quilts: General Instructions

The following instructions are not meant to be complete "how to make a quilt from scratch" information. There are already many books on that subject. The directions included here are for teaching the quiltmaker how to create historically accurate miniature quilts. Some of the information is also pertinent to large-scale projects, but the primary focus of these directions is to help the quiltmaker through the various problems that occur when working in miniature. Titles and authors of books with specific information on topics such as hand quilting and embroidery are included in the bibliography for your assistance.

PREPARATION AND PLANNING

A miniature quilt requires the same design considerations and decisions as a full-size quilt. However, if the miniature is being designed for use on a specific doll bed, some additional problems arise.

Doll beds, old and new, come in many sizes and shapes. If a realistic effect is to be achieved, the quilt must fit the bed perfectly. In other words, a well-done heirloom miniature is one which in a photograph would be indistinguishable from a large quilt. The miniature should drape and fold softly like a large quilt, should have a focal point and interest over the pillow area, and include borders that enhance and do not simply "end off" the quilt.

To make a successful miniature quilt for a doll bed, you will need to begin by making the bedding – mattress(es), pillow(s), sheet(s), pillowcase(s), blanket, etc. My students often ask me how to make these items, and for that reason I am including their instructions in this book.

MAKING MATTRESSES AND PILLOWS

Mattresses can be made from almost any fabric. I prefer ticking because of the old-fashioned look it provides. Ticking can be purchased in many different colors, or old ticking in the form of leftover scraps or coverings on old pillows can be found at yard sales. Be sure to thoroughly wash any old fabric. It is important that it be clean and without any tensile-strength damage. It is better to know that the fabric is weak and will break or tear before you begin construction of your mattress and pillow.

If a Victorian-era look is desired, then a medium or large flower print, or a striped flower design would be appropriate for the mattress covering. Plain muslin (bleached or unbleached), stripes, and similar prints would also be very suitable for certain beds and eras. Remember, the mattress really won't be seen, so the choice of covering is not critical.

Measure the base of the bed, cradle, or crib and cut a rectangle of those dimensions adding ½" to ¾" for ease, plus seam allowance. This ease will be taken up by the thickness of the mattress filling. The easiest way to make the mattress is to put the two mattress-covering fabric pieces right sides together and stitch around all four sides, leaving an opening in one side for turning. *Fig. 1.* Grade seams, turn right sides out and stuff with Polyfil® or shredded polyester batting. Quite a thick mattress can be made this way. Sometimes, however, a softer, more "real" effect can be achieved by using two thinner mattresses, rather than one super thick one.

If I'm dressing a bed which requires two mattresses, I will cut two or three layers of batting and lay them on top of the wrong side of the mattress-covering fabric.

Stitch through all layers, the same as before. Grade seams, being sure to remove as much of the batting in the seam allowance as possible. Turn right sides out and hand sew the opening closed. *Fig. 2.*

Because cradles are often quite deep, I find they usually require two and often three mattresses, each one getting slightly larger than the one below because of the slanted sides of a cradle. In order to reduce the number of mattresses, I sometimes will create a false bottom by folding cardboard in an upside-down U shape or by filling a plastic trash bag with styrofoam pellets and taping the ends closed. Pillows are made in much the same manner as the mattresses. I prefer my pillows to be firmly stuffed so they fill out the pillowcases properly.

MAKING SHEETS, PILLOWCASES, AND BLANKETS

Sheets are constructed by cutting a rectangle 5" wider and longer than the size of the completed mattress. To hem the edges, fold over the sides of the sheet ¼" and press with an iron. Repeat this step and then stitch in place either by machine or by hand. One sheet is needed to cover the mattress while a second one would serve as a top sheet and complete the look. The top sheet can be about 4" shorter than the bottom sheet as it will not need to reach up over the pillow area and tuck in. I often fold the top sheet back on itself to give a more finished look.

Pillowcases are made by cutting a rectangle twice as wide as the pillow's finished width plus seam allowance, and the length of the pillow plus seam allowance plus 1½", which will become the finished end of the pillowcase. Fold the 1½" section to the wrong side of the fabric, turn under ¼", and press. Stitch along the turned-under edge to create the pillowcase hem. *Fig. 3.* Then fold the pillowcase in half lengthwise, right sides together, and stitch along the edge and across the bottom to complete the case. *Fig. 4.* Turn right-side out.

Another method for making sheets and pillowcases is to use old linens. I especially like to use old hand towels, tea towels, and napkins. Old hand towels will often have embroidered or lace edgings, cut-work, cross stitch, embroidered designs or a lovely pattern woven

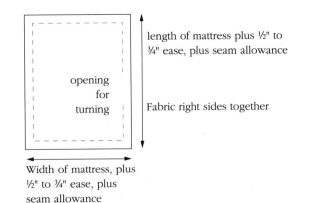

length of mattress plus ½" to ¾" ease, plus seam allowance

opening for turning

Fabric right sides together

Width of mattress, plus ½" to ¾" ease, plus seam allowance

Figure 1. *Making a mattress stuffed with polyester filling.*

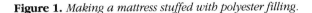

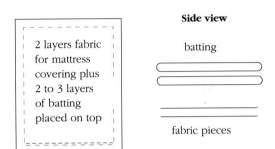

2 layers fabric for mattress covering plus 2 to 3 layers of batting placed on top

Side view

batting

fabric pieces

Fabric - right sides together.

Figure 2. *Making a soft mattress filled with layers of batting.*

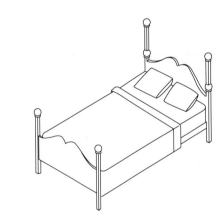

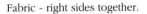

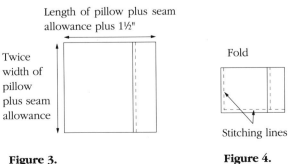

Length of pillow plus seam allowance plus 1½"

Twice width of pillow plus seam allowance

Fold

Stitching lines

Figure 3.   **Figure 4.**

Figure 5. *Hand towels.*

Figure 6. *Bed with all bed furnishings.*

Figure 7. *Same bed with quilt.*

into the linen or damask. *Fig 5.* Old linens add elegance and sophistication to your bedding, without a lot of additional needlework and time. Fortunately, hand towels are still among the less expensive items to be found at flea markets and garage sales. A blanket can be made by the same method as the sheets. A thin wool fabric would be suitable, as well as flannel material. An old adult-size blanket could be cut down to make a blanket for a doll's bed. The top edge can be bound with blanket tape found in the notions department of a fabric store. The tape may need to be cut a little narrower to keep it in scale with the blanket. Stitch the tape on by machine using a zigzag stitch. A complete set of bed furnishings will enable the quilt to drape gracefully and will complete the look of your doll's bed or crib. *Figs. 6, 7.*

PLANNING THE QUILT'S DIMENSIONS

To make the quiltmaker's job easier, I have developed a technique to produce on paper the proportions of the finished quilt. With the bedding in place, measure:

A – length of bed from headboard to footboard.

B – width of bed from side to side of mattress.

C – "tuck in" at the head of the bed, depth and width.

D – "tuck in" at the foot of the bed, depth and width.

E – distance from top of mattress to "floor" or however long you want the sides to be. *Figs. 8, 9.*

Draw each of these sets of measurements on construction or drawing paper and cut them out. Tape each section to the center section, to create a plan as shown in *Fig. 10.*

All the dimensions of the design areas of the quilt are now visible and it is easy to plan the block size necessary to fill these spaces. There will be no need to fret over whether a 3" block for the border will work; the quiltmaker only needs to look at the side areas on the plan to know the answer. This technique is not limited to making a miniature quilt for a doll bed; it works just as well for planning a miniature quilt for the wall. The only difference is that the quiltmaker, not the bed, determines the various proportions of the wall quilt.

A small quilt, like a large one, should be exciting and dynamic – as well as balanced and in proportion – if it is to be successful. By using the paper diagram technique, it is easy to plan a patchwork or appliqué pattern to fit any size doll bed or wallhanging. Of course, compromises may have to be made between the ideal pattern and the realities of the actual space; this method, however, makes those decisions easier.

FABRIC

WEIGHT AND WEAVE

Loose weaves and gauze-like fabrics are usually unsuitable for miniature work. When handling pieces of fabric 1" square or smaller, fraying can become a problem, and the additional difficulty of handling a loose weave can make your project more frustrating than fulfilling. If you insist on such a fabric for color or other reasons, then use the paper-piecing construction technique. This method stabilizes your fabric and will allow the use of a looser weave than is normally desirable.

Stay away from heavyweight fabrics such as wools and corduroys. These fabrics tend to be stiff and hard to handle when piecing or doing appliqué. In addition, the resulting quilt will be very stiff and will not drape or fold properly over a miniature doll bed. If your small quilt is for a wall, then a heavier-weight fabric might be suitable.

Do use medium-weight, good-quality, 100% cotton fabrics. These handle well and tend to have a minimum of fraying problems. If you use fabrics that are all the same weight in your quilt, your piecing and appliqué work will go more smoothly and look better.

Always wash all cotton fabric for your project in hot water with a good quality soap. I like to wash my fabrics in Orvus®, a special soap which is recommended for use on old fabrics. But no matter what soap you are using, be sure to thoroughly rinse your fabric to remove all soap residue. This residue can remain in your fabrics and cut their life span. You will be spending many hours making an heirloom miniature; don't let time destroy your work.

PRINTED DESIGN

It would seem logical that I would suggest small prints, but large prints are not to be overlooked. A quilt composed of prints that are all the same size or scale can be very boring. Large prints can provide extra interest by drawing attention to certain areas or features of the quilt. They can also add drama to the overall effect of the completed quilt. Since these quilts are small, special effects can be achieved by using the fabric's printed designs to draw attention to the quilt. A special trick

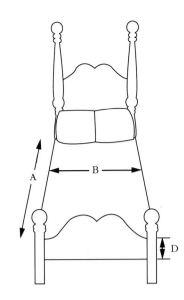

Figure 8. *Measuring your bed.*

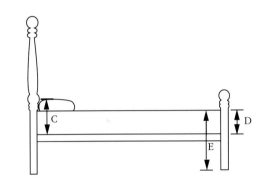

Figure 9. *Measuring your bed.*

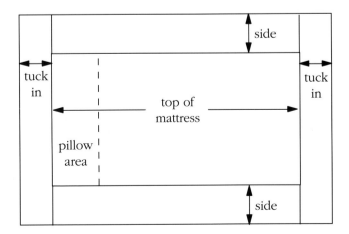

Figure 10. *Developing a plan.*

Figure 11.

available to miniature quiltmakers is to use one or two large prints to provide the look of many different fabrics. For example, if a large flower print is used, as in *Fig. 11*, and a template measuring 1" square is placed on the fabric and moved around to different areas, many different options for pattern and color emerge.

An additional advantage of using fabric this way is that all the pieces cut from the same cloth will recombine effectively in the quilt. The reason for this is simple: the manufacturer of the cloth had already designed those shapes and colors to blend together. All the quiltmaker has to do is move them around and create new shapes and patterning.

Figure 12.

Figure 13.

All types of printed designs are suitable in miniature, i.e., flower patterns, squiggly lines, geometric shapes, and wide or narrow stripes. Each of these has its own special use. Pinstripes can be used in the pinwheel pattern to make the blades appear to spin as in *Fig. 12.* Wide stripes can be cut apart to create sashings or borders, as shown in *Fig. 13.* Geometric shapes can be used to represent objects that the manufacturer never intended. *Fig. 14* shows a turkey cut from the fabric above it. *Fig. 15* shows a basket created without any piecing, and *Fig. 16* shows a vine-covered cottage

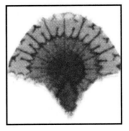

Figure 14.

Figure 15.

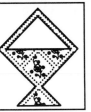

Figure 16.

made from a flowered pinstripe; the bushes around the cottage's foundation are cut from a fan-shaped print.

To help you visualize the possibilities of a piece of fabric, cut a 1" square of clear plastic and take it with you on your buying trips to the quilt store. When you get there, place the square on the fabric you are considering and move the square around the fabric's surface to see what shapes and objects you can discover. In this way, you may find that a half yard of fabric can equal many different pieces of fabric, without the additional cost.

COLOR

Keep the color scheme simple for a miniature quilt. Too many different colors within the small size of these quilts can make it difficult for the eye to focus and enjoy the design and workmanship of the quilt. But do not feel that using only two or three colors per quilt is proper, either. Often, two colors can look flat and uninteresting when used alone in a quilt.

The easiest way to determine a color scheme is to select a multicolor print fabric. This type of fabric gives the quilt a three-dimensional effect, even before the quilting is added, and can be the source of the colors used in the quilt. For example, using an overall print fabric that has green vines, flowers in two shades of salmon, blue-purple flowers, and yellow or gold centers on a light green background provides many colors that can be used throughout the entire quilt.

I do not give specific colors to use with each pattern in the "how to" section. I believe each quiltmaker should use the color choices that most please her or him. A project is more likely to be finished if it pleases its maker. If, however, you feel that you need some direction for starting your miniature, use the color photographs in the color plate section included in Part I to help you in your decision making. Be sure to include highlight and accent colors within your quilt. A miniature is not really different than a large quilt when it comes to color; the same rules apply.

CREATING AN "OLD" LOOK

The easiest way to create an "old" look is to use old fabric, fabric from the time period you wish to re-create. Antique and quilt dealers have now become aware of the public demand for old fabric, so these fabrics are readily available from dealers at quilt conventions, antique shows, antique and collectible malls, and even

flea markets. But there are two drawbacks, the first being price. The older the fabric is, the more expensive it becomes, sometimes well exceeding the cost of the new fabric needed to make a full-size quilt! Secondly, the tensile-strength of the old fabric may have deteriorated, thus causing it to tear or shatter when stitched. If you want to try to use an old fabric, wash and rinse it thoroughly, test it for colorfastness, and dry it. Carefully pull the fabric on both straight and cross grain. If it shows any signs of tearing, or if you have any doubts, don't use it!

There are other ways to get a somewhat authentic look to your quilt. Look at the fabric on your quilt store's shelves. There, among all the current fad colors, you will find centennial, late nineteenth-century, and 1930's reprints. A number of manufacturers have collections styled to accommodate the quilter who wants an "old" look. Many of these fabrics are authentic reproductions of earlier patterns and colors, and a large number of styles are available. Also available is cotton sateen, a solid color fabric that was very popular in the 1930's and 1940's because of its high sheen and low cost. It was used in both appliqué and pieced quilts. Although not always easily found today, it is still manufactured in a wide range of colors (see Resource List).

If a specific color is needed to duplicate a flower stem from 1845 or a rosebud from 1850, and your quilt store neither stocks nor has ever heard of the color, hand-dyed fabrics are available – or you can dye the fabric yourself (see Resource List).

Yet another product to assist in creating an "old fabric" look is Fading Powder®, produced by the firm By Jupiter®. This product allows the quilter to put fabric in a pot, following the directions, and cook it until varying amounts of the dye have been removed. By varying the ingredients and cooking time, the fabric can become more or less faded. Not all fabrics work well with this method, but enough do so that some wonderful soft shades can be created to make your miniature quilt look very old. The manufacturer claims the process does not damage the tensile-strength of the fabric, but to my knowledge, no long-term studies have been done.

Since tensile-strength is such an important consideration when choosing fabric, never try to use chlorine bleach to age fabric. It will severely damage the cotton fibers. Even though you may not see the damage now, time will reveal the damaging effects of such treatment.

Distressing the fabric by beating it on rocks, twisting it, and scrubbing it with hard-bristle brushes will also damage the fibers. Many quiltmakers are now experimenting with the process of overdyeing fabrics using Procion® or Rit® dyes, tea, etc. Varying degrees of color and aged looks can be achieved by all these methods. Books specific to these areas are available at your quilt shop or from many of the mail-order houses that exist to help quilters (see Resource List).

For an authentic Victorian approach to such quilt patterns as biscuits, yo-yos, and tumbling blocks, silk would be the fabric of choice. Although not readily available in all parts of the country and very expensive when it is found, silk can be obtained by visiting thrift shops and buying old ties. They often need laundering (be it dry cleaning or by hand with a mild soap). Like old cotton, not all silks will survive being revitalized, but they are a source for old coloring and patterns that can be very suitable in a miniature quilt.

TEMPLATES

I like to use plastic for my templates. I prefer the "see through" types so that I can be sure to center the designs accurately on each pattern piece. The easiest template plastic to use is the new gridded (like graph paper) type. By drafting your template directly onto this type of plastic, you can avoid transferring your pattern from graph paper to plastic. (Each time you transfer your pattern, from graph paper to template material and on to fabric, you increase the possibility of error.) By using the gridded plastic, one less chance of error occurs. But beware, all gridded plastics are not the same. Each may vary in accuracy and should be carefully measured to ensure the dimensions you want in your quilt.

Another caution: do not mix measuring instruments! All rulers are not created equal. Check each instrument before using to make sure all your equipment measures the same.

Since we are quilters, we tend to make our templates by cutting the shapes out with scissors. I find that when using scissors, there can be too much wobble or variation, so I prefer to use a craft knife and a metal ruler and over-cut each side of the template (making the cut go beyond each end of the side I'm cutting). If you do not try to cut all the way through the plastic in one cut, but rather score the lines (repeating the cut several

times), the template will drop out and be very accurate, without any nicks or bumps.

Be sure to measure and mark all templates very accurately. The width of a pencil line can be critical when working in miniature. I recommend using a mechanical pencil of 5 mm. width or finer for marking. An error of $1/16$" over only 16 pieces becomes a full 1" discrepancy, a large error on a quilt that only measures 16"!

CONSTRUCTION TECHNIQUES
ROTARY-CUTTER/STRIP-PIECING METHOD

The invention of the rotary cutter and the various types of rulers and equipment that go with it has revolutionized patchwork. No longer are tedious hours needed to cut out pattern pieces. Now, quick and accurate piecing can be achieved.

I made the Star of Bethlehem, Delectable Mountains II, Trip Around the World, Zigzag, and Thistle Cradle quilts using the rotary-cutter system. But, construction of these quilts is not limited to this technique; all could be constructed by traditional means.

To use the rotary-cutter system, first cut strips the desired width and length from your fabric as shown in *Fig. 17*. These strips are then sewn together in pairs, or larger quantities, as each quilt requires, *Fig. 18*. The

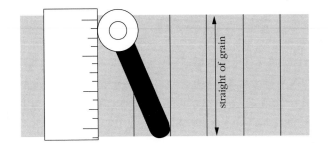

Figure 17. *Cut strips from fabric.*

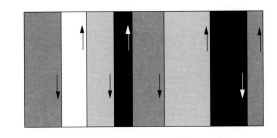

Figure 18. *Sew strips together.*

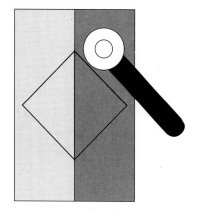

Figure 19. *Quick-cutting a pieced square.*

arrows indicate the direction of the machine stitching; by sewing alternately up and down, you can reduce warpage in the finished blocks.

In *Fig. 19,* a square template is placed over two seamed strips and the rotary cutter is used to cut out the square. If the square is placed so that the two opposite points are centered over the seam, a pieced square of two right triangles will result. This is a fast, easy, and extremely accurate way to make pieced squares in miniature.

PIECING

Whether piecing by machine or by hand, in the traditional assembly fashion or by quick-piecing techniques, I always use a standard quilter's ¼" seam. I do not trim the seams after construction, except where multiple seams come together, such as at a star point. There I grade the seams and cut off any excess. I leave the standard ¼" seams in all my quilts, because I feel they make the quilts more sturdy.

PAPER PIECING

This technique is used when precision is paramount. It takes a little extra time but guarantees a high-quality result in the completed quilt. Traditionally, paper piecing has been used when constructing hexagons or other unusual-shape pieces, but it can be used for any shape.

First, cut "papers" to the exact size of the completed patch. I find that paper is actually too thin for piecing the small pieces necessary in a miniature quilt. I prefer to use file or index cards. They are a little stiffer and hold their edge for better accuracy. I especially like the file cards that can be bought in discount chain stores.

They are a bit thinner than the ones in stationery stores and are therefore easier to stitch through.

After cutting out the "papers," cut your fabric pieces, adding the standard ¼" seam allowance to all edges. I prefer to make a plastic template for the papers and a separate template for the fabric pieces.

Place the paper in the middle of the wrong side of the fabric patch and fold the fabric edges over the paper, *Fig. 20.* The edges are then basted in place, using quilting thread for basting. I find that quilting thread is thicker and therefore easier to remove. After all the pieces are basted, assembly begins.

With right sides together, whipstitch seams together using all-purpose sewing thread in a matching color, *Fig. 21.* Try not to stitch through the papers. About 10 stitches to a half inch are adequate. After all seams are assembled, clip threads and remove basting stitches and all papers. Be careful not to clip into the fabric when removing basting stitches. Also, take care to remove all papers. If you find one when quilting the top, it will be too late to remove it!

APPLIQUÉ

The first problem that occurs when appliquéing a small piece of fabric is fraying. This difficulty can be magnified by the use of poor quality fabric. Be sure to test the fabric you intend to use for your appliqué on a piece of waste background material; then you will know whether too much fraying will develop or the fabric will be too stiff to handle. I cannot stress too strongly the importance of using a test piece. It is much easier to try a sample and discover problems than it is to find out you have committed yourself to an impossible project.

General instructions for appliqué usually specify a ¼" seam allowance. However, because of the size of the pieces to be appliquéd in miniature quilts, I recommend a seam allowance of ³⁄₁₆" to ⅛". The smaller of the two widths is used for acute angles (sharp angles), when a minimum tuck-under is all that can be successfully managed, *Fig. 22.* I cut all my appliqué pieces with the standard ¼" but trim them down as I go along, adjusting to the interaction of the different fabrics and shapes. Be careful to keep your appliqué stitches close enough together to keep all edges securely tucked under.

I favor the use of a blind-hem stitch, but an invisible stitch, buttonhole stitch, or even a very small whipstitch would also be suitable. Since these quilts are small, it is important to get a lot of three-dimensional feeling in the quilt. I do this by means of multi-layers of appliqué, the addition of embroidery stitches, or by stuffing special features.

Flawless appliqué depends on a design that doesn't ask more of the medium than it can deliver. Since seam allowances are essential for hand stitched appliqué, the surface of an appliqué at any given cross section must be wide enough to allow the seam allowances to fold beneath. Therefore, dots and thin lines must be executed by means other than fabric appliqué. Some alternatives are embroidery, crewel embroidery, painting or use of an indelible ink pen, liquid embroidery, or quilting stitches.

To correctly position appliqué, I fold my background fabric in half and press with an iron, then fold again and press, and then open and refold on the diagonals, pressing lightly. This technique will give you a center point and "lines" for positioning your appliqué pieces. *Fig. 23*. I prefer this method to marking lines with one of the dissolving chemical markers on the market. Since these markers are still new and haven't undergone the test of time, their use on an heirloom project could jeopardize its longevity.

YO-YOS: STUFFED AND UNSTUFFED

I used yo-yos on the Baltimore Album Style and Water Lilies quilts to create flowers and details. Yo-yos add a rich third dimension to the appliqué and embroidery on the quilt. The idea is not new, however; it was used on nineteenth-century quilts, especially for grapes (stuffed) and flowers (unstuffed).

A yo-yo is made by cutting out a circle, turning the edge over ⅛" and stitching through the turned-over area with a basting stitch. Use all-purpose sewing thread that matches the color of the yo-yo. The gathering thread is then drawn up tight and ended off, *Fig. 24*. After gathering, use the needle to pull the fabric out evenly into a symmetrical circle and press lightly with an iron.

If a stuffed yo-yo is desired, before completing the gathering step insert a piece of batting or polyester fill the size of a pea. Still another trick with a yo-yo is to proceed as described for the unstuffed yo-yo, but before finishing the gathering step, add a circle of contrasting color fabric to the inside of the yo-yo and end off as before, *Fig. 25*. This center circle should be the size of the completed yo-yo. If the yo-yo is to represent a

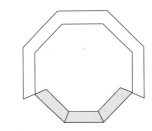

Figure 20.

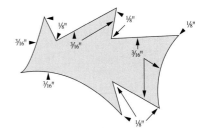

Figure 21.

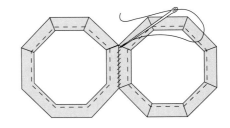

Figure 22.

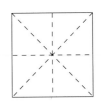

Figure 23.

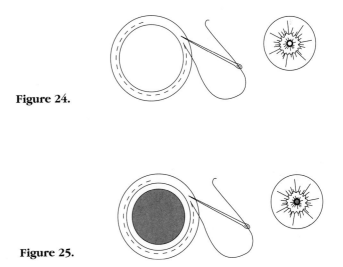

Figure 24.

Figure 25.

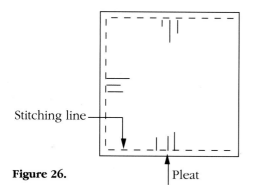

Stitching line

Figure 26.

Pleat

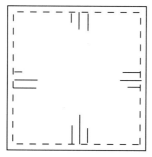

Figure 27.

Figure 28. *Baltimore Album Style Quilt, detail.*

flower, a yellow, orange, or dark green color can be used for the center circle. This will serve to look like the stamen or pistil of the yo-yo flower.

BISCUIT TECHNIQUE

To construct a biscuit from a foundation fabric (muslin or similar weight goods), cut a square of fabric the dimensions of the finished size of the biscuit plus seam allowance. Cut a larger square (exact dimensions depend on size of biscuit) from quilt fabric. Place the larger square on top of the smaller square, make a pleat on one side and pin in place; repeat on two more sides. Stitch ⅛" from the edge, *Fig 26*. Through the opening on the fourth side, stuff a small amount of polyester fill to give the biscuit its shape. Pleat this side and stitch closed, *Fig. 27*.

Assemble biscuits in rows using the full ¼" seam allowance. Biscuits are not quilted. A backing is added and the edges are finished by tucking them in or by adding lace or ruffling.

CHARM QUILTS

This type of quilt contains many different fabrics, no two of which are the same. To produce a charm quilt in miniature, all that is necessary is to collect a lot of fabric!

CONTEMPORARY QUILTS

Many of the techniques used for making large contemporary quilts – cyanotypes (sun prints), marbleizing dyeing, and embellishments – can also be used in miniature. Purchase the necessary book(s) on the subjects that interest you and simply make your project in miniature! Some of the modern techniques available in kit form are included in the Resource List at the back of this book.

EMBROIDERY

Any brand of embroidery floss will do, although I like DMC® because it has a slight sheen that adds richness to the finished project. To keep the embroidery work in a miniature quilt in scale with the appliqué pieces, I use no more than three strands of embroidery floss at a time. In the case of small stems and buds, I use only one strand. There must be variation in the size of the embroidery work, just as there is with appliqué pieces. The Baltimore Album Style Quilt is a good

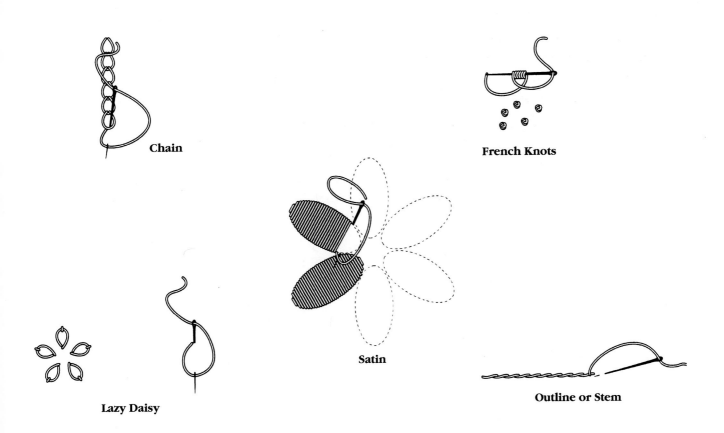

Chain

French Knots

Satin

Lazy Daisy

Outline or Stem

Figure 29. *Embroidery stitches.*

example of how the thickness of stems must contrast with that of leaves and flowers, *Fig. 28.* Some of the stitches that can be used are illustrated in *Fig. 29.*

SEWING PROBLEMS

1. *Appliqué does not turn smoothly.*

   Either too much seam allowance, or a poor choice of fabric for the appliqué, or unwashed fabric with too much sizing.

2. *Frayed edges on appliqué.*

   Too little seam allowance or too loose a weave of fabric. If the fabric choice is too loose a weave but "just right" for color or other needs, use the paper-piecing technique to stabilize the material.

3. *Seams tear out on pieced work.*

   Seam allowances are not a full ¼" or fabric has too loose a weave. The paper-piecing technique can be used instead of the traditional American seaming technique.

4. *Appliqué doesn't turn, and frays.*

   The piece you are trying to appliqué may be too small. Perhaps embroidery or another needlework technique could be used instead of appliqué.

STORING PIECES AND BLOCKS

Through teaching many miniature quilt classes and having hundreds of students, I have found a little trick I'd like to share.

Ziploc® bags must have been invented with the miniature quilter in mind. If you put all your cut-out fabric pieces in such a bag, your papers (if paper piecing) in another bag, and your completed blocks in yet a third, and then place all the small Ziplocs® into a large one you can carry your entire quilt project anywhere and everywhere without fear of losing any of your precious pieces.

I always grab my bag before leaving the house. I even keep it with me in the car. Some of us live in areas where traffic jams can last for one to two hours without any movement at all. What a satisfying feeling it is to complete quilt blocks while waiting for the traffic problem to clear!

What about doctors' offices? I always bring my bag with me and work while I await my turn. Don't forget the dentist's office, luncheons or banquets, or dull, boring meetings! Just pull out your Ziploc® bag and get to work. Don't let time be your enemy; miniatures are just perfect for busy people like ourselves.

SELECTING BATTING

When a miniature quilt is composed of many seams, such as the Star of Bethlehem or Delectable Mountains, it is more difficult for it to drape successfully on a doll's bed. Since the drape is an important part of the effect of a miniature quilt a thin batting is necessary. There are many different types on the market today. I have tried most of them.

The answer is not in any one brand of batting, but is rather in choosing the right one for the right quilt. Experimentation is the answer. The thinner and less compact the batt, i.e., Mountain Mist Quilt Light®, the easier it will be to quilt through when dealing with many seams within a small area. Others, like Pellon Fleece® and Hobbs Thermore®, which are denser but not necessarily thicker, can be very suitable for quilts where larger areas of open space are a part of the design, such as the Calimanco quilt.

Other battings with slightly more fluffy looks, such as Morning Glory® low loft, are very suitable for appliqué quilts such as the Scottie Dogs or Water Lilies quilts, where the applied motifs need some "puff" to give them character. Low-loft wool batts are now available and are easy to quilt through. Silk batting can be obtained in different styles and thicknesses. One comes in a "cap," and is very thin and unfolds to the desired size of your quilt. It is especially suited to doll-house size miniatures where an extra-thin batting is critical. The second type is sold by the meter and comes from Wales. It is a little too thick for most miniature work, but can be split in half and then you have two batts for the price of one! (See Resource List.)

There are many types of cotton batting on the market, including one new brand, Warm and Natural®, in which the cotton is needle punched into a polyester webbing for stability, allowing the quilter to not have to quilt it as closely as with the old-style batts. (If not closely quilted, a cotton batt will "wad up" during washing, creating an unevenness in the quilt). Cotton flannel would also be suitable for a miniature quilt's filler, especially if a very soft drape is desired.

Don't be afraid to experiment with various types of batts, so that you create the "look" you want in your quilt. If you should have trouble getting your quilt to successfully drape, a trick used by some people making miniature quilts may help: place no batting on the sides of the quilt; put it only on the top of the bed surface.

I use batting throughout my quilt top and have not had trouble with my quilts draping. I plan seams to come along the top edge of the mattress; this encourages the sides to fall softly. Another trick is to quilt the sides of a miniature quilt either vertically as it hangs or diagonally, forcing the quilt to drape well over the sides of the bed.

SELECTING A BACKING FABRIC

The backing of a miniature quilt deserves careful thought. It is all too easy to think that just any piece of fabric will do for the backing. In the quilts of the nineteenth century, chintzes and wonderfully interesting column prints were used. In the late nineteenth century ginghams, small calicoes (apron prints), and cretonnes were used. The backing of the quilt should relate to the quilt top in time period and color, and if a multicolor print is used, different colors of quilting threads can easily be camouflaged.

I like to use stripes for the backings of my early nineteenth-century style miniatures because they are somewhat reminiscent of the old column prints. For the late nineteenth-century pieces I often use the new reprints of the 1880's style fabrics. I like the old look they give to quilts, and the richness they provide.

PREPARING A QUILT FOR QUILTING

I always add two inches to the dimensions of a quilt top, on all sides, for both the batting and backing. By being this generous, I have allowed for any slippage that might occur in quilting (although a properly basted top should not slip during the quilting process). Also, the extra goods allow the quiltmaker using a Q-Snap® quilting frame to quilt all the way out to the edges of the quilt.

Prepare your miniature as you would a large quilt. Iron and lay out the backing. Then lay the batting on top and lay the quilt top over both. Baste through all three layers with the same care you would give a full size quilt. Don't skimp on the basting because the quilt is small. It is important to stabilize the unit for the best quilting results.

MARKING A TOP FOR QUILTING

If the quilting lines are straight, I prefer to use masking tape for marking my quilting lines, especially when filling in the background as in the Diamond in a Square or Thistle Cradle quilts. I use tape in the same width as the quilting rows, ½" or ¼", and quilt down both sides of the tape. Then I move it over to the next rows to be quilted. Be careful as you re-use the tape; it begins to stretch and warp. Once it starts to distort, discard that piece and use a new one. Remember, never leave the tape on a quilt overnight or in the hot sun (at poolside or in the car, for example), as it may leave a sticky residue. For these reasons, some quilters prefer to use drafting tape because it is less sticky than ordinary masking tape.

When marking a cable or other fancy quilting design, all the choices for marking a full-size quilt are available to the miniaturist. I prefer to stay away from the water-soluble and disappearing marking pens because of their chemical content and possible future damage to the quilt. There are many pencil and chalk type choices available. Just remember, test a small sample first to be sure the markings can be safely removed.

USING A QUILTING FRAME

I'm always asked, "Do you use a quilt frame, and if so, which one?" The answer is yes. I have used a wooden hoop and found that it stretched the miniature too much on the bias. I prefer Q-Snap® plastic frames. They come in several sizes and the pieces are interchangeable, giving the quiltmaker a lot of freedom. Because the pieces make either a square or rectangular frame, the quilt is not as easily pulled off grain and will hang straight when finished. Be sure to put the frame on the quilt with sides parallel to the edges of the quilt. And, as mentioned earlier, this type of frame allows the quilter to work out to the very edge of the quilt, thereby enabling the same quilting tension to be kept throughout the quilt.

QUILTING

From the very first planning of a miniature quilt, or of any quilted work, consideration should be given to the quilting. Since these quilts are small and some pat-

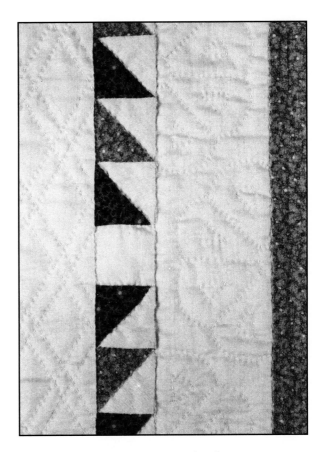

Figure 30. *THISTLE CRADLE QUILT, detail.*

terns contain hundreds of pieces, there are many seams, which mean extra-hard work when quilting.

If I want a lot of quilting, I plan my miniature quilt to have as large areas as possible for the quilting. An example of this is the Thistle Cradle quilt, *Fig. 30.*

If I want a feature of a quilt to be more distinctive, I will often choose to do some stipple quilting in that area, to cause that feature to stand out. Such a quilt was the Sunburst where the background area in the center circle has been stippled to make the printed motif more dominant. The quilting in this area is in concentric rows so very close together, ¹⁄₁₆" to ⅛", that the entire area is flattened and the unquilted areas – the flowers – pop up and appear stuffed.

When quilting a miniature with many seams, like Delectable Mountains, the best approach is to use the "quilt in the ditch" method. When the quilt is being constructed, care must be taken to press all seams to one side, instead of open. The side of the patch that has the seam pressed beneath it will appear higher than the side of the patch without seam allowance. Quilt along this lower side, next to but not in the seam itself. Quilting in the seam can weaken it.

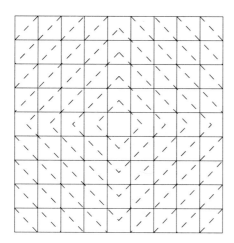

Figure 31. *Quilting stitches.*

Another method that makes quilting many seams more bearable is to quilt through the center of each patch, forming concentric diamonds or squares. I used this technique in my Trip around the World quilt, *Fig. 31*. This technique minimizes the seams one has to quilt through; however, it does not eliminate them.

Since seams are a problem in miniature quilts, one is tempted to forego large amounts of quilting. I think this approach is in error. It is the quilting that makes a quilt a quilt. And it is the quilting that adds depth and dimension to any patchwork or appliqué design. Since the purpose is to capture the look and essence of old quilts, it is important to remember that the originals were heavily quilted. To duplicate them effectively, as much quilting as possible should be included in the miniature.

When quilting a miniature with small appliqué such as Scottie Dogs or the Baltimore Album Style quilt, or when embroidered vines or stems are next to the quilting, be sure to consider the proportion between the quilting stitches and the needlework. Not everyone can quilt small enough (18 stitches or more to the inch) to keep the quilting stitches in scale to the appliqué or embroidery. Whenever I'm faced with this problem, I usually choose to quilt close to the edge of the small work so that the quilting isn't immediately noticeable. The result is that I have provided the needed quilting without confusing the eye as to which it should focus upon – the design or the quilting. Quilting around the shapes causes them to puff up or "pop-out" and draw the attention they deserve.

I find it confusing to the eye when contrasting color quilting thread is used. I always match my quilting thread to the background area or patch that I am quilting. This way the quilting becomes secondary to the design surface of the quilt, as in many full-size quilts, and allows the viewer to enjoy the graphics of the quilt first, and the beauty of the quilting second.

TYING

Originally many quilts were not made as bedspreads or counterpanes, but as "blankets" for warmth – for strictly utilitarian purposes. As a result, many quilts received no quilting, but instead were tied. Wool yarn was used to make knots at even intervals across the quilt to hold the three layers together. There is no reason not to apply this technique to a miniature quilt. I have used it on hexagon quilts.

Sometimes I like the ties to show and do knotting on the front as in Grandmother's Flower Garden with three strands of embroidery floss, *Fig. 32*. Other times, as in the case of the Elongated Hexagon quilt, I use the ties only to hold the layers together and use one or two strands of floss, knotting on the reverse side where it won't interfere with the graphic design of the top.

USING DIFFERENT FINISHING TECHNIQUES

A. *Backing brought to the front:*

Bring the backing fabric over the front edge of the quilt and tuck the edges of the backing under to form a ¼" wide binding, trimming backing fabric as necessary. For a professional look, miter all binding corners.

B. *Edges tucked in:*

Turn front and back edges of quilt to the inside and slipstitch the folded edges together. Lace or ruffling can be added before the edges are stitched closed.

C. *Separate bias binding applied:*

This method of edge-finishing is my favorite – not because it is the easiest technique, but because it looks the best. It allows me to create a binding that is in better scale with the proportions of a miniature quilt. Be sure to cut the bias strips on the true bias. I use the see-through plastic rulers with a 45° angle marked on them. I cut my bias strips ¾" wide and machine stitch them onto the front of the quilt in a ⅛" seam. Several strips will need to be cut and pieced together to form one strip long enough to bind off the quilt. Bring the binding over the edge, fold in seam allowance and hand stitch in place using a blind-hem stitch, *Fig. 33*. A successful binding is the same width along all sides, is smooth, and is filled with batting.

D. *Piping:*

Insert piping in between the front and back edges of the quilt. I have seen this technique used on quilts from the mid and late nineteenth century. Be sure to keep the piping in scale with the size of the quilt. There is packaged small piping commercially available for use on baby clothes that would suit certain miniature quilts.

E. *Scalloped edges:*

These were popular in the 1920's and 1930's. They can be achieved in miniature if care is taken in planning. Use either bias binding or edge finishing technique B to complete the edges.

F. *Prairie points:*

Points can be carefully folded to be in proportion to a miniature quilt's edge.

G. *Old lace or tatting:*

These edgings can be used to simulate the handmade fringe of the late eighteenth- and early nineteenth-century quilts. Many of these quilts were white-on-white counterpane types that would look excellent on four-poster doll beds. This style of edging is also appropriate for Victorian novelty quilts, such as biscuit, crazy, and yo-yo quilts.

H. *Hand-loomed tapes:*

Hand-loomed tapes were used on late eighteenth- and early nineteenth-century quilt edges. They were usually narrow bands, about ½" to ⅝" wide, that were stitched over the raw edges of the quilt. This method can be emulated in miniature by the use of seam binding (preferably the older type which is quite thin and has a looser weave). Trim the quilt to even the edges and apply the seam binding over both the top and back surface of the quilt, using a running stitch. End by cutting off the end of the binding ½" longer than needed, folding the raw edge to the inside, and slipstitching the end of binding edge over the beginning edge.

Any edge or finishing treatment used on a large quilt can be used on a miniature – just remember to keep it in scale with your quilt.

SIGNING AND DATING

I'm a firm believer in signing and dating all quilts and quilted objects. How easy our quilt heritage

Figure 32. *Grandmother's Flower Garden, detail, showing ties on the surface of the quilt.*

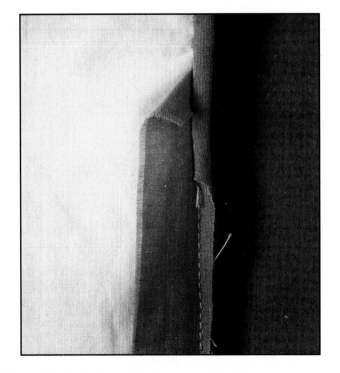

Figure 33. *Beginning and ending area of binding.*

Figure 34. *Quilts signed and dated in embroidery.*

research projects would be if all quiltmakers of the past had signed and dated their quilts. There is no reason not to sign your work. Be proud of what you have produced, and if your work is a gift, the recipient will be proud to have your name on it.

I always put my name, the date, a copyright symbol if appropriate, and the number in the series on the back of each quilt, no matter what the size. Some quilts are embroidered with the information, *Fig. 34.* Others have it written in indelible ink on a separate label. I prefer, when possible, to mark directly on the quilt; a separate label can always get lost.

In order to further document my work, I keep a 5½" x 8" three-ring notebook with my original graphs, fabric swatches, and all pertinent information, such as beginning and completion dates, number in the series, photo of quilt. This log will afford future historians a wealth of information, not only about the quilt but also about its maker, and it will provide me with documented proof for my insurance company in event of an accident or theft.

It only takes a few minutes to write down the facts while you are making a quilt. It can take ever so much longer if you wait until after the quilt is complete to try to remember all the information you will need to write in your log. So, stop right now and buy a three-ring notebook for documenting your work! Future historians will thank you.

Part III

Making the Quilts: Projects & Patterns

*Please Read General Instructions
Before Attempting to Make
Any of the Following Patterns*

Figure 35. *Whole Cloth.*

WHOLE CLOTH
Color Plate I

Dimensions: 14½" x 19½"
Number of Pieces: 1
Construction Technique: Not Applicable.
Fabrics: Glazed chintz, polished cotton, or cotton sateen. A contrasting backing fabric will make the quilt reversible.

DIRECTIONS:

Beginning in the center, mark the quilt top using the patterns provided. See quilting diagram, *Fig. 36,* for placement. Remember to reverse left and right side patterns. Quilt from the center out.

Complete quilt using Finishing Technique C.

YARDAGE:

⅝ yd. – top
⅝ yd. – backing

CUT:

1 rectangle 14½" x 19½" – top
1 rectangle 17" x 22" – backing

Figure 36. *Quilting diagram.*

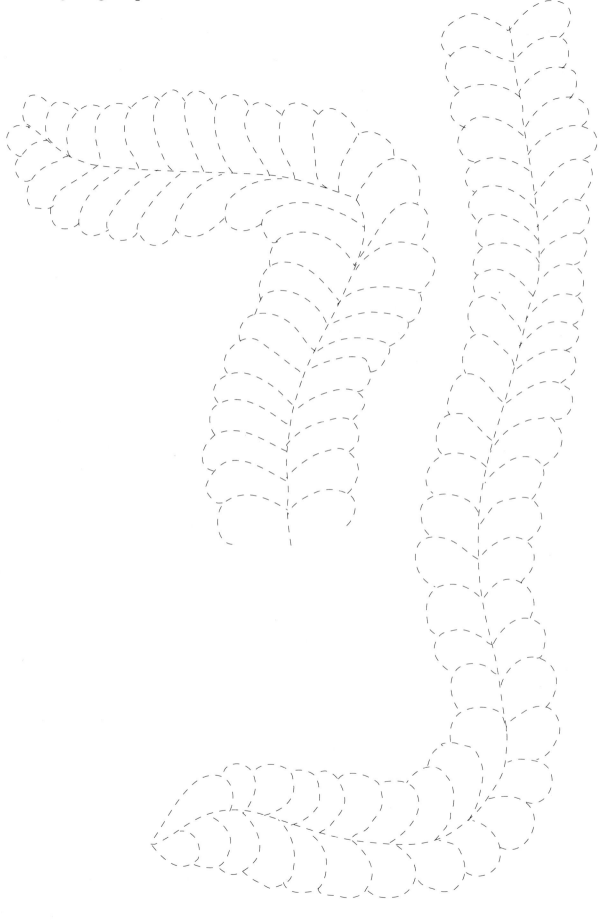

Figure 37. *Sunburst.*

SUNBURST
Color Plate II

Dimensions: 19½" x 19½"
Number of Pieces: 60
Construction Techniques: Pieced over paper and by machine; appliquéd.
Fabrics: All types of prints are suitable. Contrast in color value is needed for good definition of sunburst rays. If you are using a stripe for the borders, the finished dimensions of the quilt will depend upon the width of the stripe chosen.

DIRECTIONS:

Cut fabric pieces using the templates on page 43. Use paper-piecing technique. Assemble B to C to form unit shown in *Fig. 38*. Join units to circle A. Add D segments to complete the sunburst. See assembly diagram, *Fig. 39*.

Appliqué sunburst to background square. Cut away backing from behind circle, leaving a ¼" seam. Clip basting and remove papers.

Add borders, mitering corners.

YARDAGE:

¾ yd. – A and borders (in order to accurately match stripes)
¼ yd. – B
¼ yd. – C (if centering flowers – 18 repeats are needed)
⅜ yd. – background
⅝ yd. – backing

CUT:

1 of A
18 of B
18 of C
18 of D

1 – 13½" square of the background
4 – 22" strips the width of the stripe (suggested width 3", 3½", or 4" maximum), matching stripe pattern in all four pieces.
22" square of the backing

Figure 38.

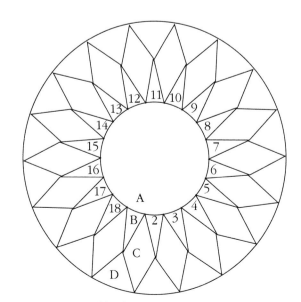

Figure 39. *Assembly diagram.*

Quilting: Quilt center circle around pattern in stripe, filling background with stippling, if desired. Quilt ¼" inside innermost rays, diamonds, and pie wedges. Background is quilted in three parallel rows ¼" apart around circle. The rest of the background can be filled with three parallel rows ¼" apart, measured from border edges. The remaining areas are filled by continuing to quilt in ¼" parallel rows: Quilt borders in ¼" parallel rows from the center out. See *Fig. 40* for quilting diagram.

Complete quilt using Finishing Technique H or C.

Figure 40. *Quilting diagram.*

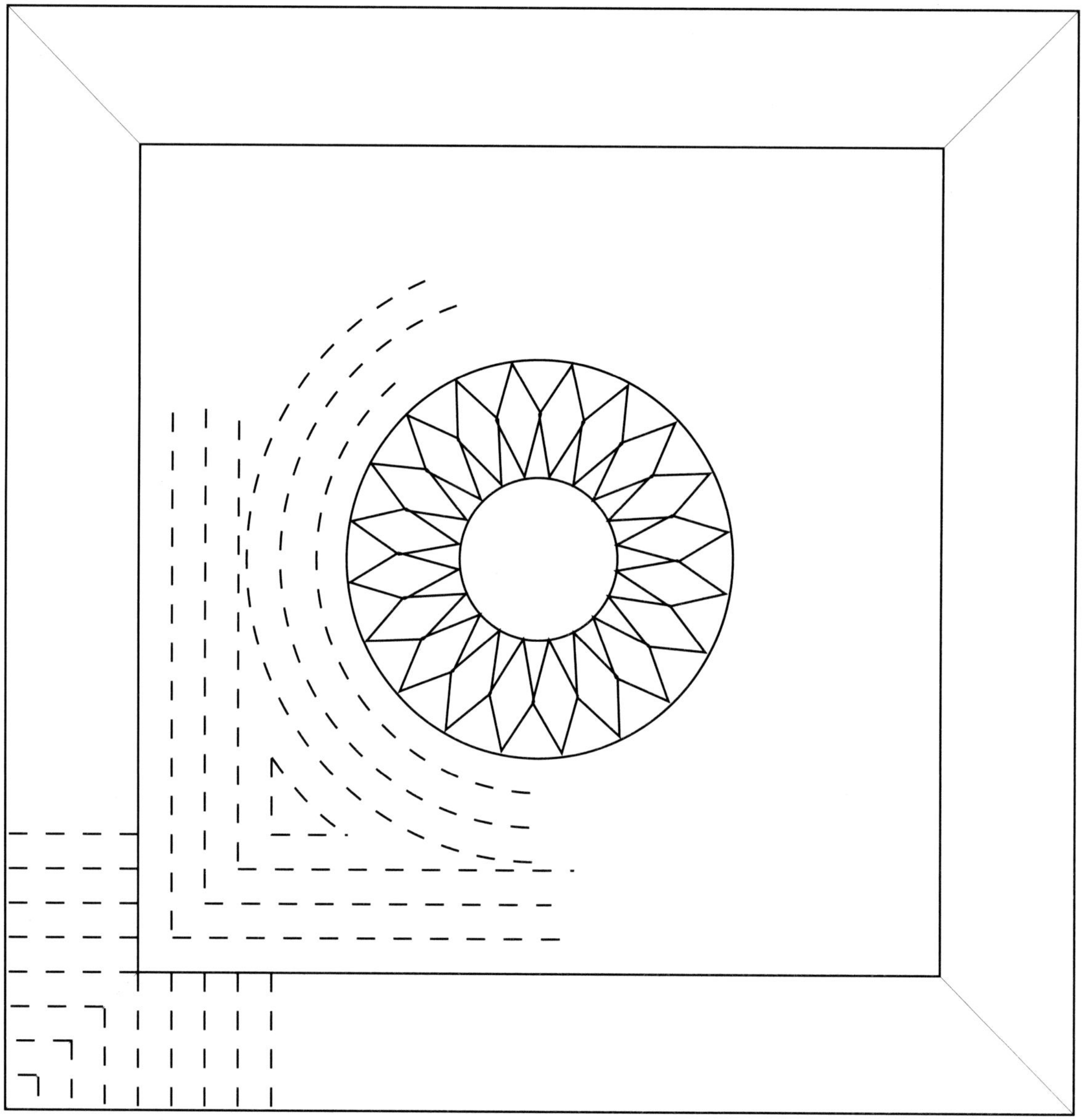

42

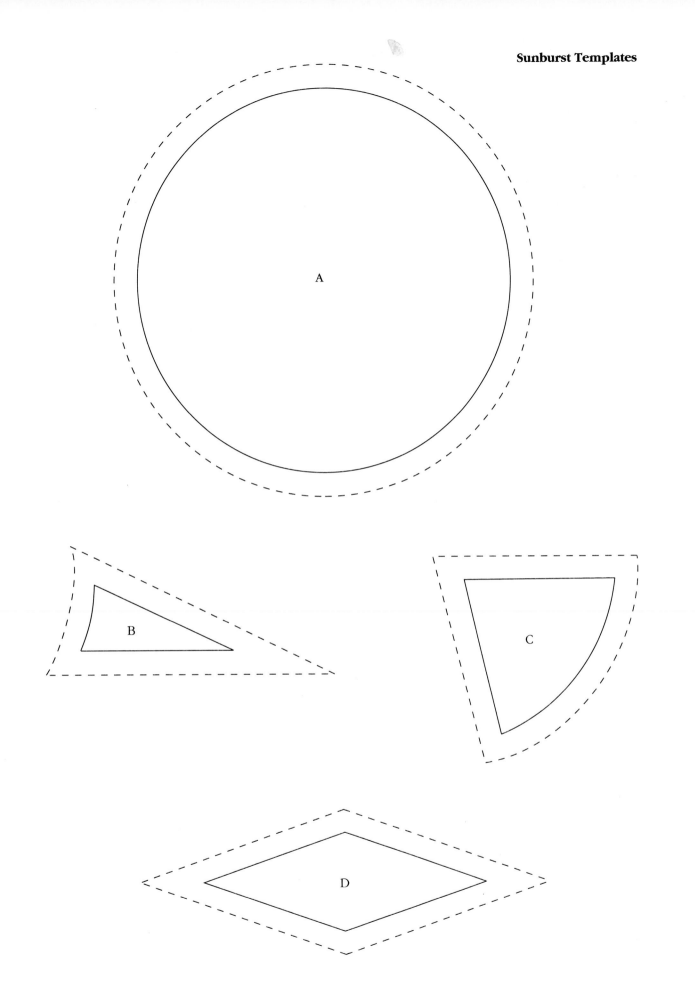

A

B

C

D

Figure 41. *Bethlehem Star.*

YARDAGE:

¼ yd. – A/K (dark)

¼ yd. – E/I (dark)

¼ yd. – J (dark)

¼ yd. – F (medium dark)

¼ yd. – C (medium)

¼ yd. – H (medium)

¼ yd. – B/G (medium light)

¼ yd. – D (light)

¾ yd. – backing (add extra yardage to C if separate binding is to be applied)

CUT:

For Large Star:

1 – 24" x 1¼" strip of each: A, B, C, D, E, F, G, H, I, J, K

For Small Star:

4 – 13" x 1" strips of B and C

8 – 13" x 1" strips of F

For Half Stars:

4 – 13" x 1" strips of B and K

Background:

Cut after large star is assembled; see Directions.

Borders:

4 – 23" x 1" strips of B (inner borders)

4 – 26" x 1¼" strips of C (outer borders)

Backing: Cut 4" larger than quilt top.

BETHLEHEM STAR
Color Plate III

Dimensions: 24" square

Number of Pieces: 516

Construction Techniques: Machine pieced and hand appliquéd.

Fabrics: 8 different. To achieve a soft gradation with distant "rings" use:

3 dark, 1 medium dark, 2 medium, 1 medium light, and 1 light.

DIRECTIONS:

Be sure to cut and piece with care and accuracy.

Construct 6 fabric units as follows:

#1 – ABCDEF

#2 – BCDEFG

#3 – CDEFGH

#4 – DEFGHI

#5 – EFGHIJ

#6 – FGHIJK

Stagger assembly of rows as in *Fig. 42.*

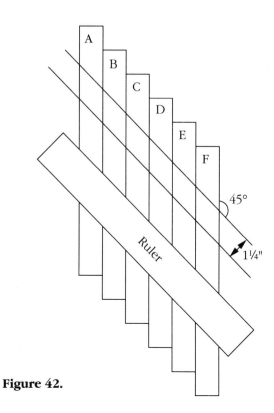

Figure 42.

To create the star's rows, cut across each fabric unit at 1¼" intervals, eight times at a 45° angle. Being careful not to stretch the bias edges as you assemble, sew one cut section from each fabric unit to the next in sequence as in *Fig. 43*, to form a large diamond, *Fig 44*.

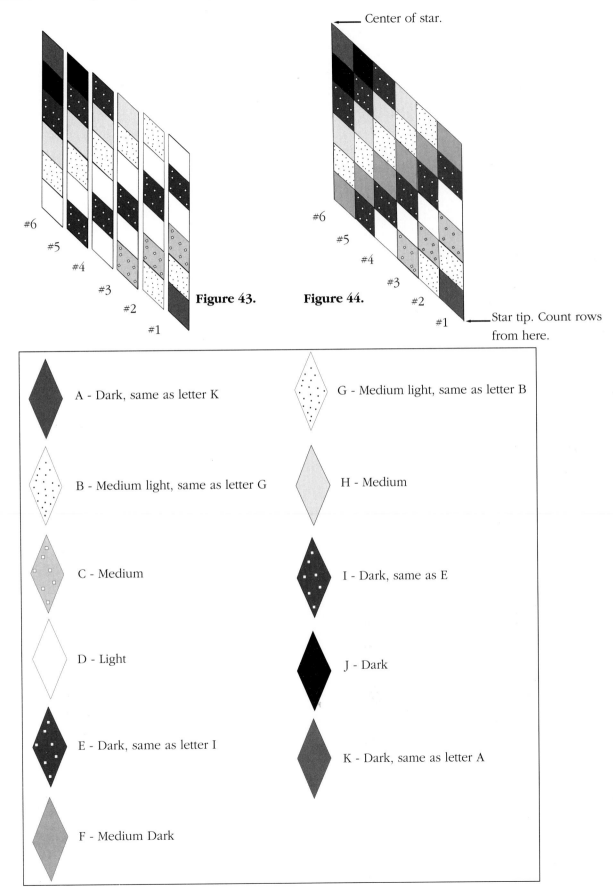

Center of star.

Figure 43.

#6
#5
#4
#3
#2
#1

Figure 44.

#6
#5
#4
#3
#2
#1

Star tip. Count rows from here.

A - Dark, same as letter K

B - Medium light, same as letter G

C - Medium

D - Light

E - Dark, same as letter I

F - Medium Dark

G - Medium light, same as letter B

H - Medium

I - Dark, same as E

J - Dark

K - Dark, same as letter A

The resulting diamond is one of the eight "legs" of the large star. Assemble all eight large diamonds and then sew them into pairs, *Fig 45*. Then sew two pairs into one-half of the star, and repeat to form the other half.

When sewing the two star halves together, the precision of your work will be evident and the star will either lie flat or create a large mountain. If the latter happens, you must remeasure your seams and adjust any that are inaccurate.

Assemble the small and half stars in the same manner as the large stars. Rows are cut at 1" intervals for both the small and half stars. See *Fig. 46* for fabric unit assembly of small stars and *Fig. 47* for half stars.

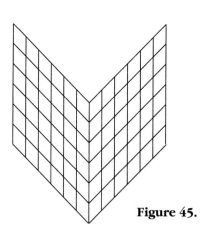

Figure 45.

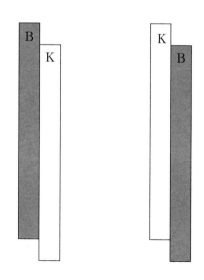

Figure 46.

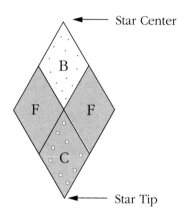

Star Center

Star Tip

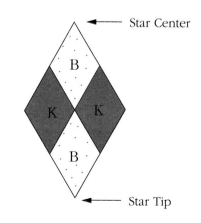

Star Center

Star Tip

Figure 47.

Cut background fabric 2" larger than large star. Appliqué star onto background, being sure to keep legs at a 90° angle to each other and adjacent point tips parallel, *Fig. 48.*

Appliqué small stars within corner squares and half stars between legs of stars. Cut away background fabric from behind stars, leaving ¼" seam allowance, and trim background square to ¼" beyond large star tips.

Add inner border using ¼" seams and miter corners. Add outer border and miter corners.

Quilting: Large Star: quilt all pieces "in the ditch" along seam lines.

Corner Stars and Half Stars: Quilt in the same way as in the large star and fill in spaces between with quilted stars and triangles, as in *Figs. 49 and 50.*

Finish the quilt using edge Finishing Technique A or C.

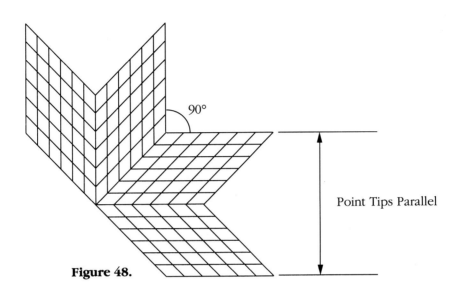

Figure 48.

90°

Point Tips Parallel

Figure 49.

Fig. 50. *Quilting diagram.*

47

Figure 51. *Indigo Blue & White.*

YARDAGE:

¾ yd. – background and backing

¾ yd. – A, D

⅜ yd. – B, C, E, F, G, H and binding

CUT:

10 of A

10 of B

16 of C

2 of D

2 of E, 2 of F (inner borders)

2 of G, 1 of H (outer borders). Use inner border template and *Fig. 53* as guides.

19" x 23¼" rectangle of background fabric

21" x 25" rectangle for backing

INDIGO BLUE & WHITE
Color Plate IV

Dimensions: 19" x 23¼"

Number of Pieces: 45

Construction Technique: Appliqué.

Fabrics: 1 dark blue print, 1 medium blue print, white for background

DIRECTIONS:

Mark the 3½" borders on all sides of the background rectangle. Divide the 12" center width into four equal sections of 3" each. Divide the 16½" length into five equal sections of 3½" each.

Using layout diagram, *Fig. 52*, begin by appliquéing the bottom row of trees in the center motif area. These should be ⅛" above the base line you have drawn so as not to bleed into inner Sawtooth border area. Next, appliqué the tree row above and continue in like manner until all five rows have been completed. Using the markings you have made as a placement quide, appliqué inner border in place.

Next, appliqué outer border trees lining up the base of three stems with the edges of the quilt, see *Fig. 52*. Appliqué outer Sawtooth borders, being careful to cover the trunks of the trees.

Quilting: Quilt around each tree motif and Sawtooth. Using quilting templates provided (page 50), quilt birds with circle over small trees in center area. Quilt circle between trees in outer border. Using appliqué template C as a quilting pattern, quilt the tree motif in top border area as if appliquéd trees existed there. Remember to quilt circles between these trees also; see *Fig. 52*.

Complete quilt using Finishing Technique C.

48

Figure 52.

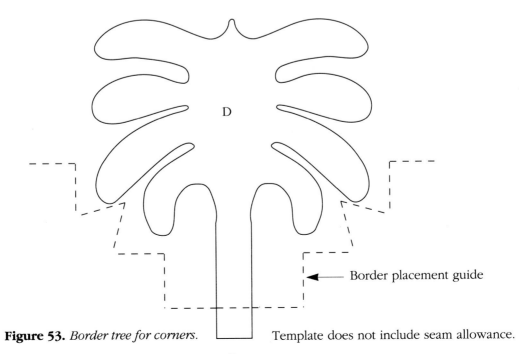

Figure 53. *Border tree for corners.*   Template does not include seam allowance.

Border placement guide

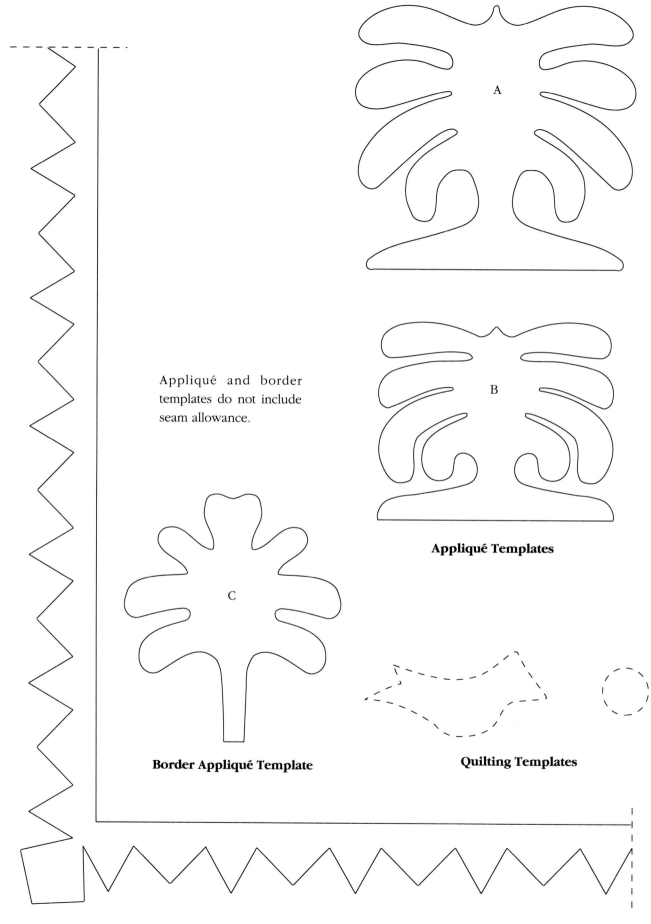

Appliqué and border templates do not include seam allowance.

A

B

Appliqué Templates

C

Border Appliqué Template

Quilting Templates

Border Template

50

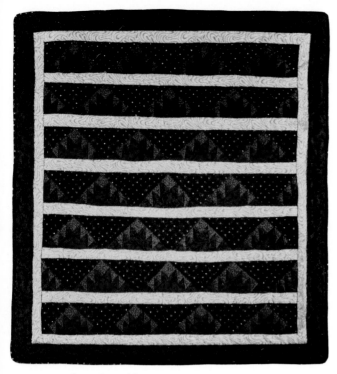

Figure 54. *Delectable Mountains.*

YARDAGE:

⅜ yd. of A, B, and binding

⅜ yd. of C, D, G, and outside borders

¼ yd. of E, F

¼ yd. of sashing and inside borders

⅝ yd. of backing

SKILL LEVEL: *Intermediate*

DELECTABLE MOUNTAINS
Color Plate V

Dimensions: Approximately 14½" x 16"

Number of Pieces: 388

Construction Technique: Pieced, hand or machine.

Fabrics: Any combinations are suitable. Contrast needed
to define Sawtooth imagery.

CUT:

If using the "quick-piece" method of construction for
Sawtooth blocks:

3 – 1" x 40" strips of D

3 – 1" x 40" strips of E

If not using the "quick-piece" method:

112 – D

112 – E

PLUS (for both methods):

24 – A

8 – B

25 – C

25 – F

56 – G

6 – H

6 – I

6 – J

2 – 13" x 1" strips, 2 – 14" x 1" strips (inner borders)

2 – 15" x 1¼" strips, 2 – 16½" x 1¼" strips (outer borders)

Delectable Mountains detail

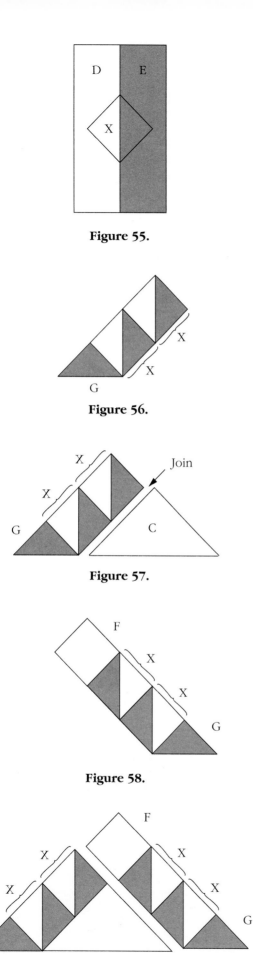

Figure 55.

Figure 56.

Figure 57.

Figure 58.

Figure 59. *Block #1.*

DIRECTIONS:

If quick piecing, seam each D strip to an E strip. Cut 112 one-inch squares from joined strips, *Fig. 55.* If using templates, sew a D triangle to an E triangle and make 112 one-inch squares. Join squares together into pairs.

To make block #1, join patch G to the left side of a pair of X blocks, as shown in *Fig. 56.* Sew this unit to left side of C, *Fig. 57.* Add F to left side of a second pair of X blocks and join G to the right side of this unit, *Fig. 58.* Sew this unit onto the other side of C, as shown in *Fig. 59.* Construct 24 more blocks in a like manner.

For block #2, stitch an H to the left side of a pair of X blocks and a G to the opposite end, see *Fig. 60.* Join this unit to an I, *Fig. 61.* Construct two more blocks in a like manner. Repeat entire process, reversing order for left side of quilt block #2. Assemble rows as shown in the assembly diagram, *Fig. 62.*

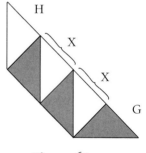

Figure 60.

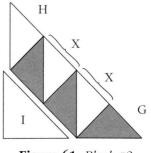

Figure 61. *Block #2.*

Use care in all aspects of assembly. Not only is accuracy necessary for all seams, but caution must be exercised when assembling rows because the large A triangles are likely to stretch on the bias, causing the sashings J to become too short. If you recheck all your measurements and seams and J is still too short, recut it to match your row's measurement. Add J to the base of all rows. Assemble Row #1 starting with a B triangle, to Row #2 starting with Block #2; continue assembling the top, alternating rows. See the assembly diagram, *Fig. 62*.

Attach shorter inner border strips to top and bottom rows; longer inner border strips to sides. Miter all corners. In the same manner attach outside borders and miter corners.

Quilting: Quilt "in the ditch" around all pieces. Using quilting patterns provided, quilt in each A and B segment. Quilt chain motif in outside borders.

Complete quilt using Finishing Technique C or A.

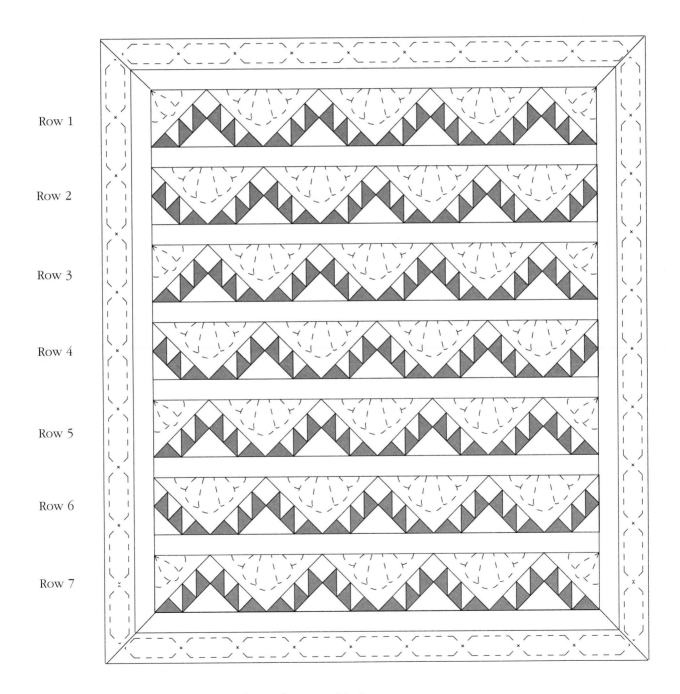

Figure 62. *Assembly diagram.*

Figure 62a. *Assembly Diagram for Rows*

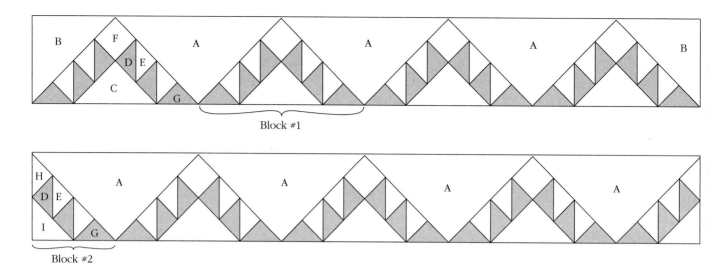

Block #1

Block #2

Delectable Mountains Templates

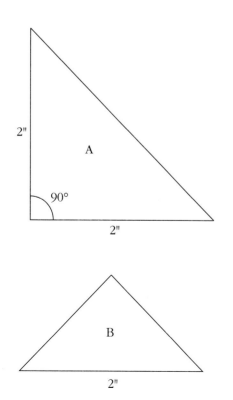

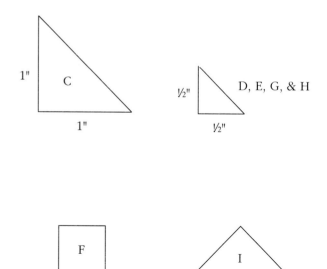

Templates Do Not Include Seam Allowance.

Templates Do Not Include Seam Allowance.

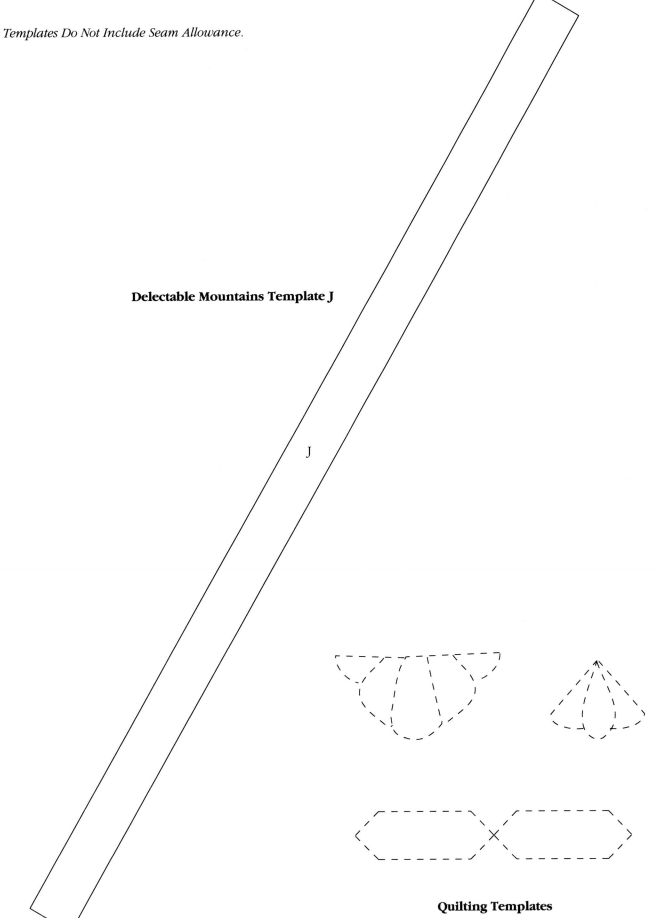

Delectable Mountains Template J

J

Quilting Templates

Figure 63. *Baltimore Album Style Quilt.*

YARDAGE:

Assorted scraps

¼ yd. – of each primary color (i.e. red and green)

¼ yd. – border swags

¼ yd. – sashings

⅝ yd. – background

¾ yd. – backing

½ yd. – binding (if not finishing the edges by bringing the back over the front)

CUT:

Number of each pattern piece as labeled.

From background fabric:

25 – 4" squares

4 – 2¾" x 27" strips for borders

From sashing fabric:

20 – 1" x 4" strips

4 – 1" x 17½" strips

4 – 1½" x 19½" strips for outside sashings (inner borders)

From Backing Fabric:

1 – 27" square

BALTIMORE ALBUM STYLE QUILT
Color Plate VI

Dimensions: 26½" x 26½"

Number of Pieces: 157

Construction Techniques: Appliquéd, pieced, embroidered.

Fabrics: Choose at least two colors to be carried out throughout quilt, i.e. red and green for continuity. I used six different greens (five prints and one solid) and three different red prints. This miniature is an excellent scrap quilt and the use of many different prints and solids enriches the finished quilt. Medium to dark fabrics provide the best contrast with the light background. Don't forget the occasional light fabric for contrast against a dark one.

Embroidery Floss: Light and medium green, dark red, dark and medium pink, black, brown, medium and dark yellow and/or gold, and purple.

DIRECTIONS:

It is best to begin with whichever block seems least complicated to you. #5 & #21 have the largest areas of uninterrupted curves, and #19 & #7 contain gentle turnings and simple embroidery. Use either the iron-pressing method in the General Instructions or lightly mark each square with a chalk pencil to ensure accurate placement of appliqué and embroidery. After you have completed several blocks, the remaining ones will seem less complicated and will not be as difficult to undertake. Antique Baltimore Album quilts were personal statements of the quiltmakers of the mid-nineteenth century. Your quilt should reflect your interest and skills. Do not hesitate to repeat a block you like. Make it in several different color combinations, vary the size of the flowers in a vase or the basket. Make this quilt your own.

In a block requiring both appliqué and embroidery, always do the appliqué first. More accurate placement of embroidery designs can be achieved this way. Round flowers are more easily constructed if a yo-yo is made first. It can be attached either with the gathered side down and hidden under the round upper surface or with the gathered side up, thus adding sculptural interest to your flowers.

Embroidery: Main stems and wreaths should be worked with two strands of embroidery floss. Smaller stems and details should be worked using a single strand. By varying the thickness of floss, the concept of main stems versus bud or leaf stems will be more easily defined.

Use:

Outline or Stem Stitch:

stems

detailing on lyre, cornucopia and vases

pineapple's crosshatching

Declaration of Independence outline

Satin Stitch:

leaves, calyxes, buds, tulips, and roses

peacock's tail

cornucopia fruit

Independence Hall's windows, cupola, chimneys, and weathervane

tassels on swag border

Chain stitch:

wreaths, basket handle

larger flower stems

Lazy Daisy Stitch:

flowers in blocks #7, 8, 14, and 18

French Knots:

cherries, grapes

some of the flower centers

peacock's eye and crown

Pineapple's crosshatching centers

Permanent Marker, very fine point:

Declaration of Independence wording

When the blocks have been completed, assemble in horizontal rows, as in *Fig. 64,* alternating them with 4" sashing strips. Assemble rows and attach to long sashing strips; continue until all 25 blocks have been sewn together. Add outer border strips and miter corners. Appliqué swags to outer borders and embroider tassels.

Quilting: The quilting should be kept simple. Outline quilting or "quilting in the ditch" is recommended for the pattern shapes and along the sashing and border seams. Following the shape of each swag, quilt two or three rows inside each.

Complete quilt using Finishing Technique A or C.

Baltimore Album Style Quilt detail

Figure 64. *Assembly diagram.*

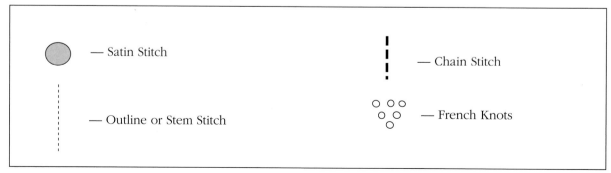

Embroidery Key

Border Template

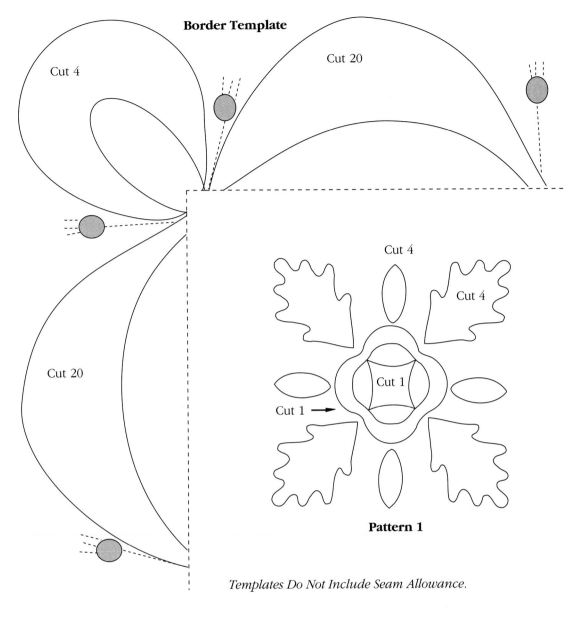

Cut 4

Cut 20

Cut 20

Cut 4

Cut 4

Cut 4

Cut 1

Cut 1 →

Cut 20

Pattern 1

Templates Do Not Include Seam Allowance.

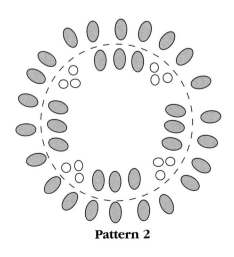

Pattern 2

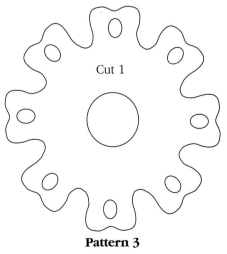

Cut 1

Pattern 3

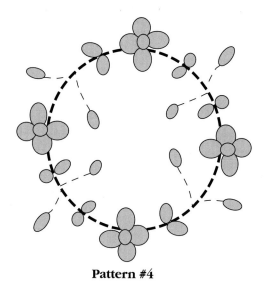

Pattern #4

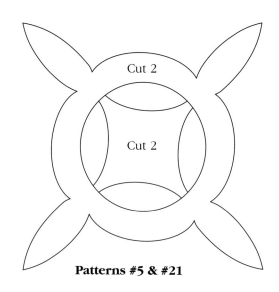

Patterns #5 & #21

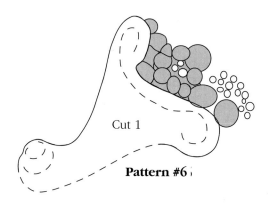

Pattern #6

Templates Do Not Include Seam Allowance.

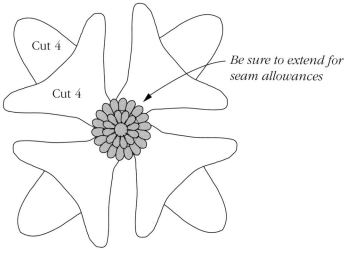

Be sure to extend for seam allowances

Pattern #7

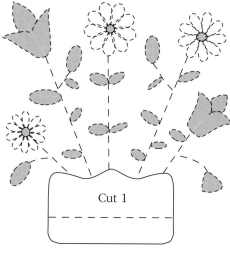

Pattern #8

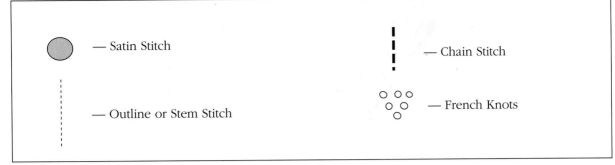

Embroidery Key

Templates Do Not Include Seam Allowance.

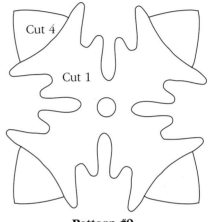

Pattern #9

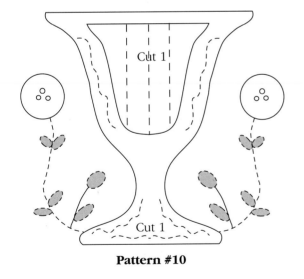

Pattern #10

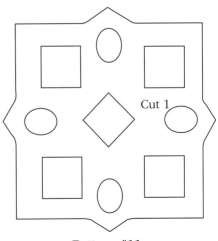

Pattern #11

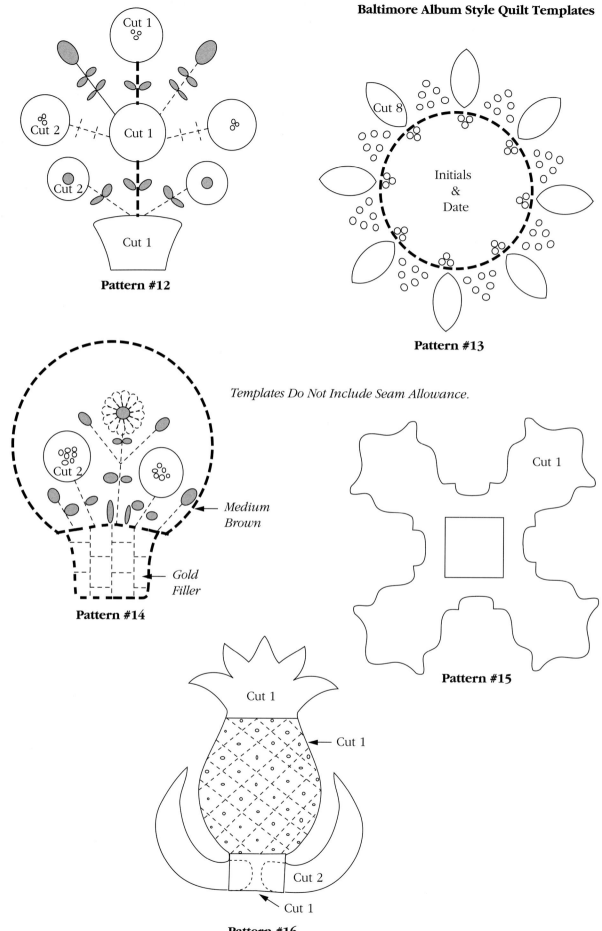

Cut 1

Cut 2

Cut 2

Cut 1

Pattern #12

Cut 8

Initials
&
Date

Pattern #13

Templates Do Not Include Seam Allowance.

Cut 2

→ *Medium Brown*

→ *Gold Filler*

Pattern #14

Cut 1

Pattern #15

Cut 1

Cut 1

Cut 2

Cut 1

Pattern #16

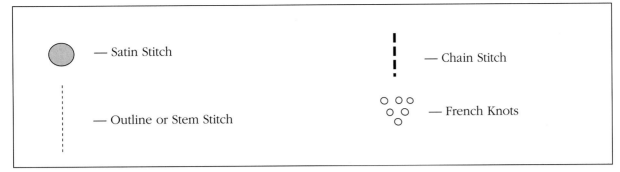

Embroidery Key

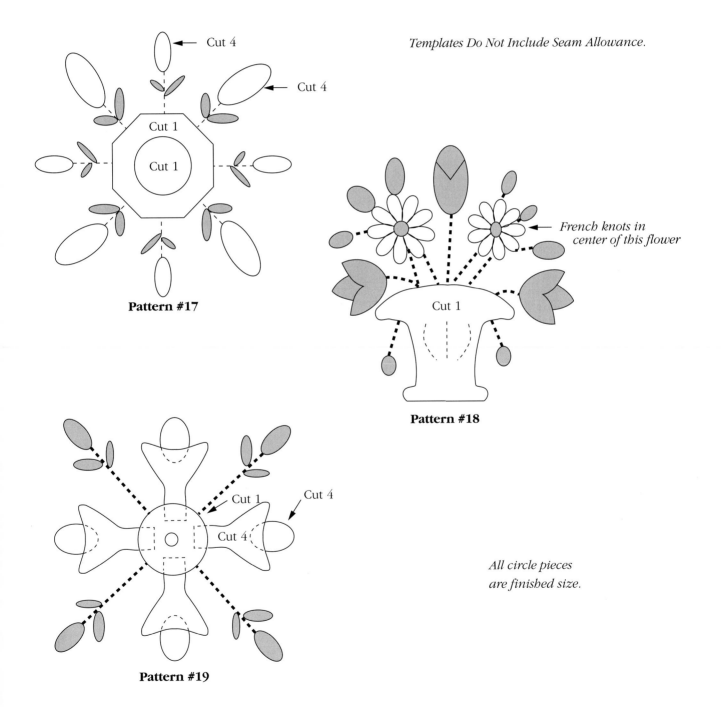

Templates Do Not Include Seam Allowance.

Cut 4

Cut 4

Cut 1

Cut 1

Pattern #17

French knots in center of this flower

Cut 1

Pattern #18

Cut 1

Cut 4

Cut 4

Pattern #19

All circle pieces are finished size.

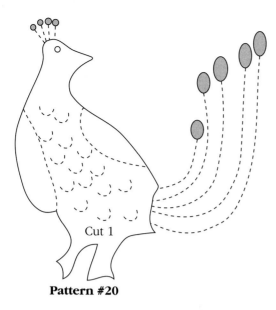

Pattern #20

Templates Do Not Include Seam Allowance.

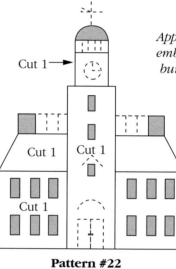

Cut 1 →

Appliqué and then embroider. Order of appliqué: building, roof, tower.

Cut 1

Cut 1

Cut 1

Pattern #22

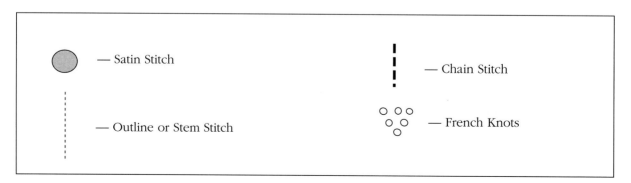

— Satin Stitch

— Chain Stitch

— Outline or Stem Stitch

— French Knots

Embroidery Key

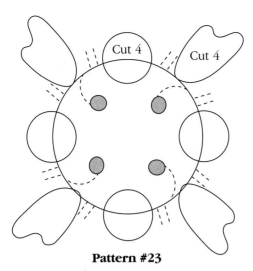

Pattern #23

*Cut 1 of white and appliqué,
then embroider.*

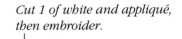

Templates Do Not Include Seam Allowance.

Pattern #24

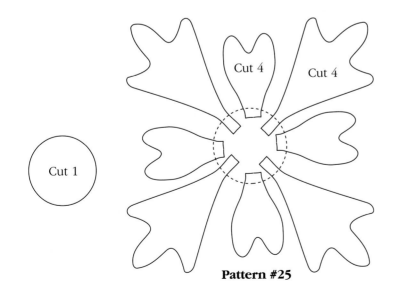

Pattern #25

Figure 65. *Union Quilt.*

YARDAGE:

5 different ¼ yd. pieces for A (if binding is to be made
   from A, then ⅜ yd. is needed)

5 different ¼ yd. pieces for B

¾ yd. – background, outer borders and backing
   or

⅜ yd. – background and outer borders
   and ⅝ yd. – backing

CUT:

6 – A of each different fabric, total 30

6 – B of each different fabric, total 30

30 – 3½" squares from background fabric

2 – 17" x 1" strips, 2 – 20" x 1" strips (inner borders from
   one of the "B" fabrics.

2 – 18" x 1¼" strips, 2 – 22" x 1¼" strips (outer borders)

1 – 20" x 23" rectangle, backing

SKILL LEVEL: *Beginner*

UNION QUILT
Color Plate VII

Dimensions: 18" x 21"

Number of Pieces: 68

Construction Techniques: Appliquéd and pieced.

Fabrics: Stripes, ticking, Americana prints in red, white
   and blue.

DIRECTIONS:

Fold each background square in half lengthwise and
press. Along fold line, position the tip of the shield A ½"
above bottom edge. Appliqué in place, being careful to
keep stripes straight (parallel to the edges of the background square). Next appliqué shield top B, positioning
tip along fold line ½" from top edge, *Fig. 66.*

Assemble shields into rows. See *Fig. 67.* Join rows.
Add inner borders and miter corners. Add outer borders
and miter corners.

Quilting: Quilt around shield pieces and "in the ditch"
along each block's seams and along border seams.

Complete quilt by using Finishing Technique C.

Figure 67. *Assembly diagram.*

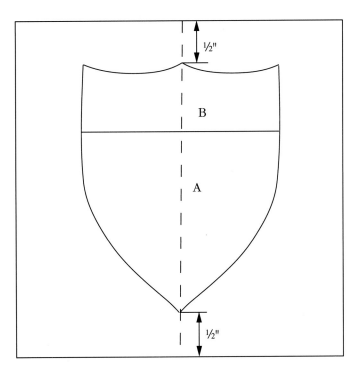

Figure 66.

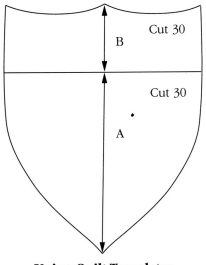

Union Quilt Templates

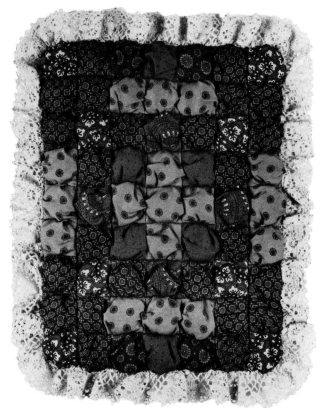

Figure 68. *Biscuit Quilt.*

YARDAGE:

Scraps or:

⅛ yd. of A

⅛ yd. of B

⅛ yd. of C

⅛ yd. of D

⅛ yd. of E

⅛ yd. of F

¼ yd. of muslin

⅜ yd. of backing (or fat quarter)

1 yd. of gathered lace

Stuffing, i.e. loose polyester, dacron, etc.

CUT:

63 – 1½" squares muslin

8 – 2" squares A

24 – 2" squares B

17 – 2" squares C

4 – 2" squares D

4 – 2" squares E

6 – 2" squares F

1 – 8" x 10" rectangle – backing

SKILL LEVEL: *Beginner*

BISCUIT QUILT
Color Plate VIII

Dimensions: 9" x 11"" (includes lace trim)

Number of Pieces: 126

Construction Technique: Machine pieced.

Fabrics: Silk, cotton lawn, or any lightweight cotton. Muslin for biscuit foundation.

DIRECTIONS:

Make biscuits as described in the General Instructions. Assemble into rows using assembly diagram, *Fig. 69.* Hand or machine-stitch lace to biscuits.

Complete quilt using Finishing Technique B.

Figure 69. *Assembly diagram.*

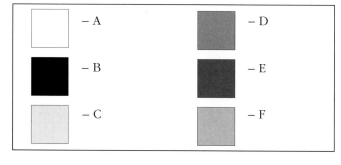

Assembly Key

68

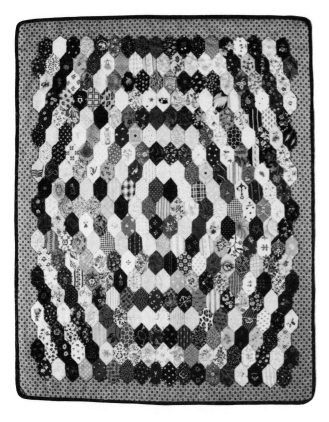

Figure 70. *Elongated Hexagon Charm.*

YARDAGE:

Scraps only

⅝ yd. – borders and backing

CUT:

182 – dark hexagons

169 – light hexagons

1 – 15" x 19" rectangle for borders

1 – 17" x 21" rectangle for backing

351 papers

ELONGATED HEXAGON CHARM
Color Plate IX

Dimensions 15" x 19"

Number of Pieces: 351

Construction Technique: Paper piecing.

Fabrics: Strongly contrasting lights and darks. Because this is a charm quilt, no two pieces are to be the same. In trying to achieve a late nineteenth-century look, be sure to include some novelty prints, i.e. cats, dogs, scissors, flags, etc.

Embroidery Floss: 1 skein for tying quilt.

DIRECTIONS:

Fold fabric over papers and baste, as described in the General Instructions. Starting with a light-colored hexagon, surround it with dark hexagons to form an elongated rosette. Continue around the rosette by alternating light and dark rows until the top is completed; see the assembly diagram in *Fig. 71*.

Appliqué hexagons to border rectangle. Cut away excess fabric from behind hexagons, leaving ¼" seam allowance. Because of all the seams, no batting is necessary. The quilt will drape more softly without it. I did choose to put a thin batting in mine, to create a slightly puffier look.

Tie with triple-strand embroidery floss in square knots on the reverse of the quilt.

Complete quilt using Finishing Technique A or C.

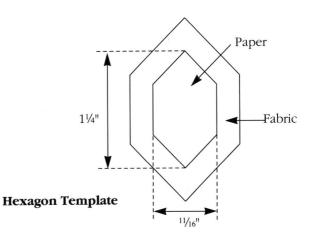

Hexagon Template

Figure 71. *Assembly diagram.*

Figure 72. *Trip around the World.*

TRIP AROUND THE WORLD
Color Plate X

Dimensions: 21" x 21"

Number of Pieces: 293

Construction Techniques: Pieced, hand or machine.

Fabrics: Prints or solids in any color combinations are suitable – include some strong contrasting fabrics. (I used 10 different fabrics.)

DIRECTIONS:

Using either the "quick-piecing" technique or the individual template method, assemble the blocks and rows using *Fig. 73* as a guide. Add borders and miter corners.

Quilting: Quilt on the diagonal through each color to accentuate the "trip" effect; see *Fig. 74*.

Using quilting pattern provided on page 73, quilt a double cable in the border.

Complete the quilt using Finishing Technique C or A.

YARDAGE:

SCRAPS OR:

⅛ yd. of A (dark)

⅛ yd. of B (medium dark)

⅛ yd. of C (medium)

⅛ yd. of D (medium dark)

⅛ yd. of E (light)

⅛ yd. of F (dark)

⅛ yd. of G (medium)

⅛ yd. of H (dark)

⅛ yd. of I (medium)

¼ yd. – borders

⅝ yd. – backing

CUT:

Using 1" square template:

5 – A

12 – B

20 – C

28 – D

36 – E

44 – F

52 – G

60 – H

32 – I

4 – 22" x 2¼" strips for borders

1 – 22½" square for backing

Trip around The World Template

1" square

Template does not include seam allowance.

A	B	C	D	E	F	G	H	I	H	G	F	E	D	C	B	A
B	C	D	E	F	G	H	I	H	I	H	G	F	E	D	C	B
C	D	E	F	G	H	I	H	G	H	I	H	G	F	E	D	C
D	E	F	G	H	I	H	G	F	G	H	I	H	G	F	E	D
E	F	G	H	I	H	G	F	E	F	G	H	I	H	G	F	E
F	G	H	I	H	G	F	E	D	E	F	G	H	I	H	G	F
G	H	I	H	G	F	E	D	C	D	E	F	G	H	I	H	G
H	I	H	G	F	E	D	C	B	C	D	E	F	G	H	I	H
I	H	G	F	E	D	C	B	A	B	C	D	E	F	G	H	I
H	I	H	G	F	E	D	C	B	C	D	E	F	G	H	I	H
G	H	I	H	G	F	E	D	C	D	E	F	G	H	I	H	G
F	G	H	I	H	G	F	E	D	E	F	G	H	I	H	G	F
E	F	G	H	I	H	G	F	E	F	G	H	I	H	G	F	E
D	E	F	G	H	I	H	G	F	G	H	I	H	G	F	E	D
C	D	E	F	G	H	I	H	G	H	I	H	G	F	E	D	C
B	C	D	E	F	G	H	I	H	I	H	G	F	E	D	C	B
A	B	C	D	E	F	G	H	I	H	G	F	E	D	C	B	A

Figure 73. *Assembly diagram.*

A – Dark

B – Medium light

C – Medium

D – Medium dark

E – Light

F – Dark

G – Medium

H – Dark

I – Medium

Assembly Key

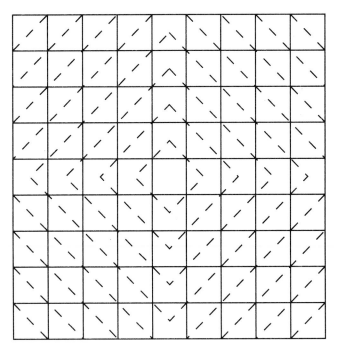

Figure 74. *Quilting diagram, detail.*

Double Cable Border

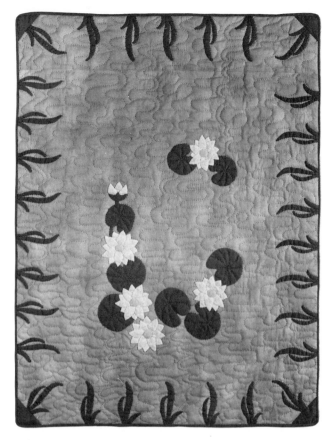

Figure 75. *Water Lilies.*

YARDAGE:

½ yd. – lily pads, reeds, calyx, bud stem, corners and
  binding

⅛ yd. – flower petals

scraps or ⅛ yd. – flower centers

¾ yd. – background and quilt backing

CUT:

5 – A

3 – B

30 – C

31 – D

2 – E

1 – F

5 – G

30 – H

30 – I

30 – J

4 – K

1 – ½" x 2¾" bias strip (bud stem)

1 – background 20" x 26"

1 – backing 21" x 27"

WATER LILIES
Color Plate IX

Dimensions: 20" x 26"

Number of Pieces: 172

Construction Technique: Hand appliqué.

Fabrics: Cottons, cotton sateens, hand-dyed fabrics
  (especially for water).

DIRECTIONS:

First, locate, mark, and baste bud stem, calyx, and lily
pads onto background; see *Fig. 76*

Appliqué pattern pieces in the following sequence:
bud stem, bud petal D, petals E, and calyx F. Next
appliqué all lily pads. To form each lily apply under-
petals D first, then upper-petals C on top; see assembly
diagram. Complete each flower with the center G made
from a yo-yo, either stuffed or unstuffed; see General
Instructions.

On the outermost area of the quilt, locate, mark and
baste all reed leaves. For proper placement use assembly diagram, *Fig. 76*. Last, appliqué corner triangles K
in place.

Quilting: Using the quilting pattern provided on templates A and B, quilt lily pads in matching color quilting
thread. Quilt around each flower center and all petals.
Quilt the background in a free-form ripples pattern; see
suggested design on page 76. Fill entire background.
Quilt around all lily pads, stems, and reeds.

Complete quilt using Finishing Technique C.

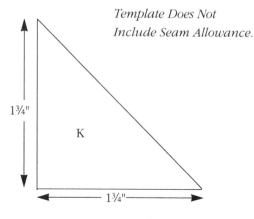

Corner Template

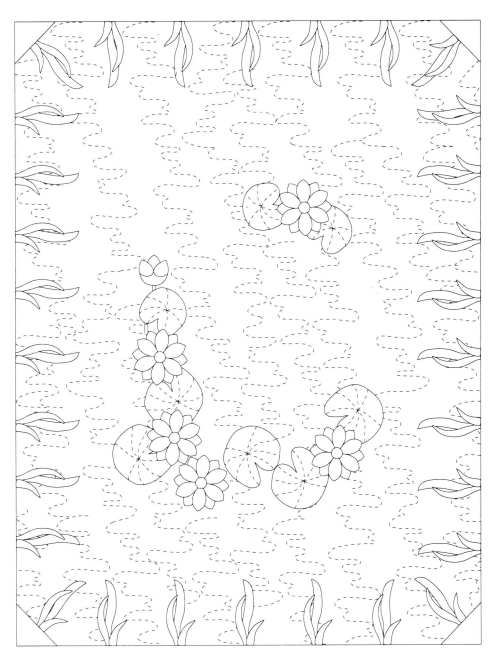

Figure 76. *Assembly diagram.*

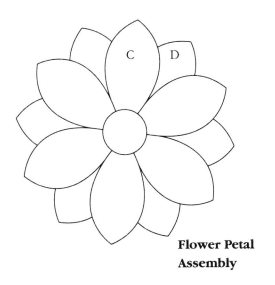

**Flower Petal
Assembly**

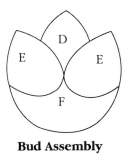

Bud Assembly

75

Water Lilies Templates

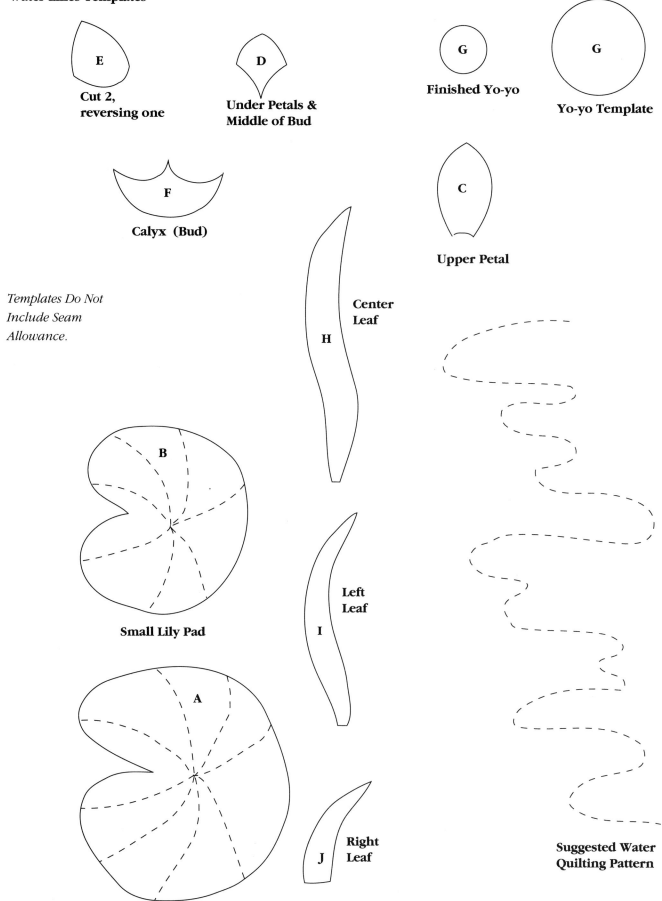

E

**Cut 2,
reversing one**

D

**Under Petals &
Middle of Bud**

G

Finished Yo-yo

G

Yo-yo Template

F

Calyx (Bud)

C

Upper Petal

*Templates Do Not
Include Seam
Allowance.*

**Center
Leaf**

H

B

Small Lily Pad

**Left
Leaf**

I

A

Large Lily Pad

**Right
Leaf**

J

**Suggested Water
Quilting Pattern**

Figure 77. *Grandmother's Flower Garden.*

YARDAGE:

scraps (not less than a 3½" x 10½") of 24 different prints
scraps of 24 different solids
⅛ yd. of a solid color for single hexagon between paths
1¼ yds. of muslin for hexagons and backing

CUT:

12 hexagons from each print
2 hexagons from each solid color:
except for the 35 hexagons from solid color chosen for
   single hexagon between paths
438 hexagons from the muslin
809 papers
After top is assembled, cut backing rectangle 1" larger
   than top.

GRANDMOTHER'S FLOWER GARDEN
Color Plate XII

Dimensions: 21⅞" x 25½"
Number of Pieces: 809
Construction Technique: Paper piecing.
Fabrics: Lightweight cottons, cotton lawn, silk, hand-
   dyed cottons.
Embroidery Floss: To match solid color fabrics, except
   the muslin.

DIRECTIONS:

Fold fabric over papers and baste as described in the
General Instructions. Assemble prints and coordinating
solids into rosettes. There will be a pair of each color
rosette. Join rosettes to paths in rows, placing a solid-
color hexagon between paths where the rows join. See
Fig. 78.

After top is assembled, cut backing and place a very
thin batting between layers. Using a square knot, tie
with three strands of embroidery floss in each of the
rosette's center hexagons and solid color hexagons
between the paths.

Complete the quilt using Finishing Technique B.

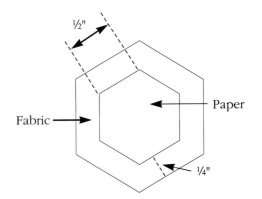

Grandmother's Flower Garden Template

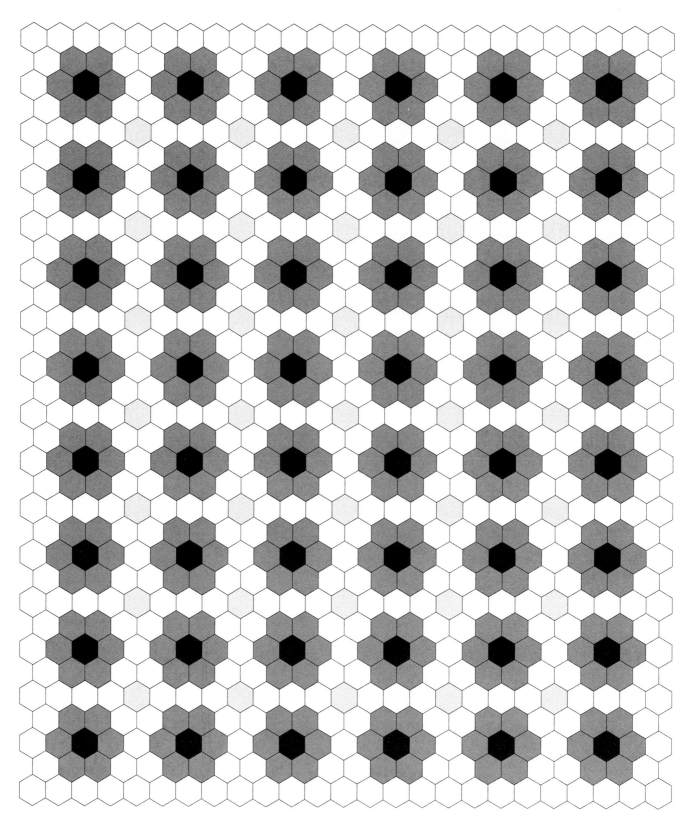

Figure 78. *Assembly diagram.*

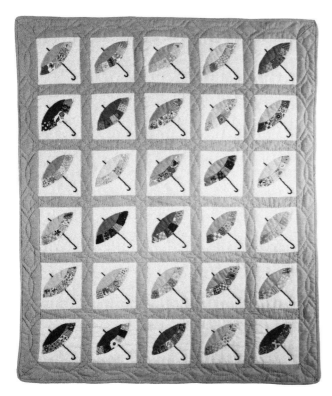

Figure 79. *Umbrellas.*

YARDAGE:

Scrap; for a charm quilt:

180 different prints

30 different solids

⅜ yd. – background

⅜ yd. – sashings and borders (½ yd. if making bias binding)

¾ yd. – backing

CUT: *From fabric:*

30 – A

30 – B

30 – C

30 – D

30 – E

30 – F

30 – G

30 – 3½" squares

24 – 1¼" x 3½" strips, 5 – 1¼" x 19½" strips (sashings)

2 – 1½" x 21½" strips, 2 – 1½" x 25¼" strips (borders)

Backing: 22½" x 26¼" rectangle

UMBRELLAS
Color Plate XIII

Dimensions: 20½" x 24½"

Number of Pieces: 273

Construction Techniques: Paper piecing and appliqué.

Fabrics: Cotton scraps, cotton sateen, bleached muslin.

Embroidery Floss: 1 skein black.

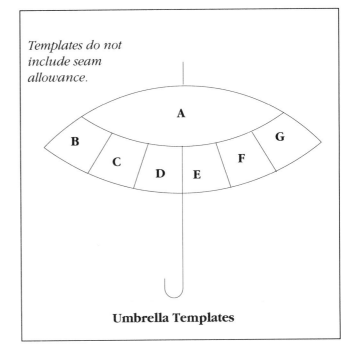

Umbrella Templates

From paper:

30 – A

30 – B

30 – C

30 – D

30 – E

30 – F

30 – G

DIRECTIONS:

Fold fabric over papers and baste as described in General Instructions. Assemble lower umbrella pieces B, C, D, E, F and G, joining side seams. Stitch completed unit to top A.

Fold background squares as indicated in *Fig. 80* and press with an iron. Place the umbrella (with the papers still inside) so that the tips are on the fold lines and equidistant from the edges of the square. Check to be sure that the center umbrella seam is on the 45° fold. Appliqué the umbrellas to the background squares. Cut away background fabric from behind umbrella, leaving ¼" seam. Clip basting and remove papers.

Using two strands of embroidery floss, embroider umbrella tip and handle in outline or stem stitch, along the fold line, *Fig. 80*.

In laying out squares for assembly, try to arrange the colors to balance left to right and top to bottom.

Stitch short sashings to umbrellas to form rows of five blocks across. Attach a long sashing to the bottom of the first row and to the next four rows. Stitch rows together, as in the assembly diagram, *Fig. 81*. Add borders and miter corners.

Quilting: Quilt around umbrellas, handles, and tips. Using quilting patterns provided, quilt sashings and borders.

Complete quilt using Finishing Technique C or A.

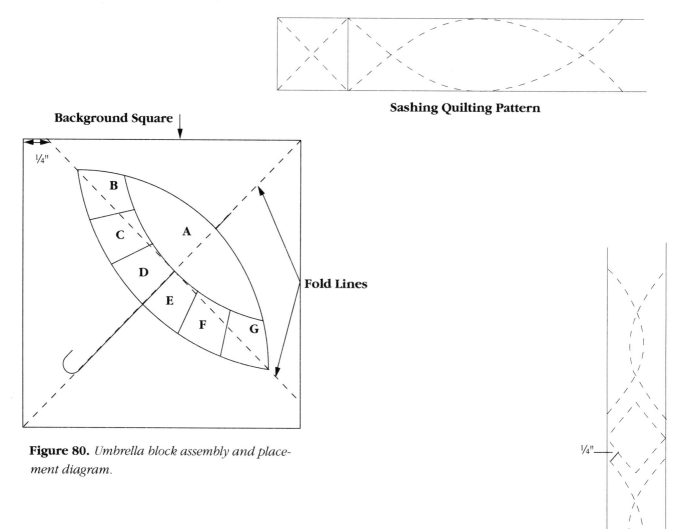

Sashing Quilting Pattern

Figure 80. *Umbrella block assembly and placement diagram.*

Border Quilting Pattern

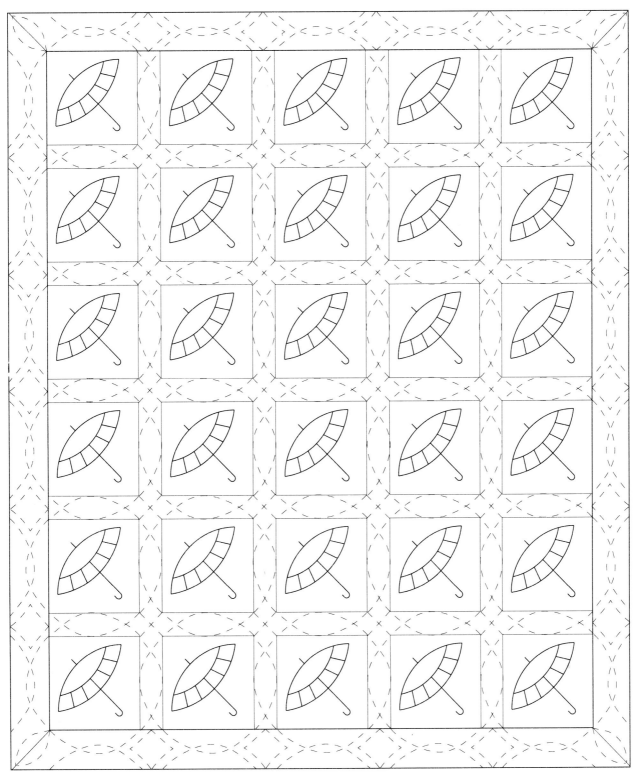

Figure 81. *Assembly diagram.*

Figure 82. *Scottie Dogs.*

YARDAGE:

scraps – enough to make two Scotties from each
¼ yd. – inner border
¼ yd. – outer border
½ yd. – background and backing
¼ yd. – binding (same as one pair of Scotties)

CUT:

24 – 12 pairs Scotties (one of each pair facing left, and
  one facing right)
2 – 14" x 1¼" inner border strips
2 – 20" x 1¼" inner border strips
2 – 16" x 1¼" outer border strips
2 – 22" x 1¼" outer border strips
1 – 12½" x 18½" rectangle – background
1 – 17" x 22" backing

SKILL LEVEL: *Beginner*

SCOTTIE DOGS
Color Plate XIV

Dimensions: 15½" x 21½"
Number of Pieces: 32
Construction Technique: Appliqué.
Fabrics: 12 different fabrics: 1930's reprints, checks,
  plaids, and geometrics.

DIRECTIONS:

Using assembly diagram, *Fig. 83*, mark (with a removable marker, such as chalk) the 3" grids on the background rectangle. Locate and position scotties using black-and-white photo and layout diagram, taking care to balance color and patterning. Baste Scotties in place. Appliqué. Add inner borders, mitering corners. Do the same for the outer borders.

Optional: Add embroidered eyes or other details.

Quilting: Quilt along the 3" grid lines and around each dog and border seams.

Complete quilt using Finishing Technique C.

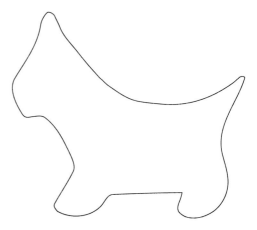

Scottie Dogs Template

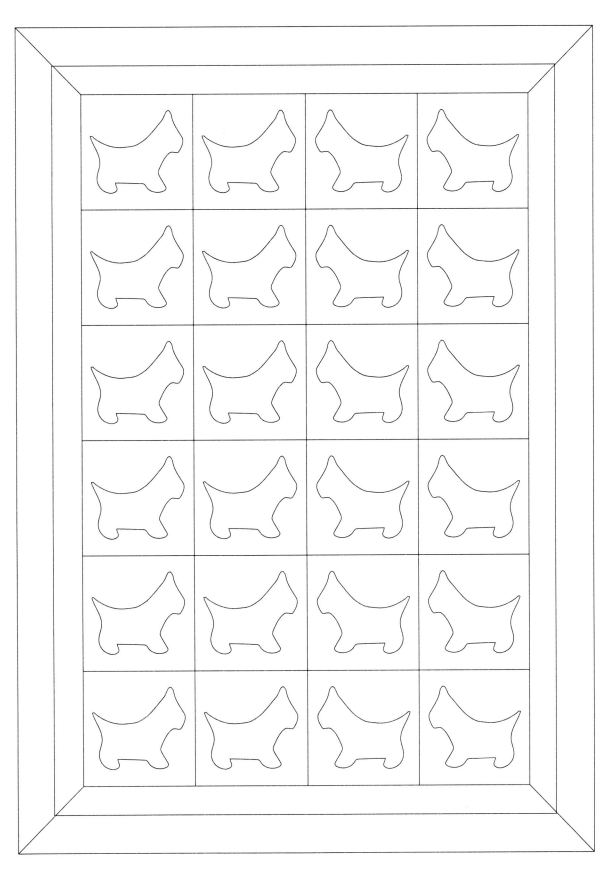

Figure 83. *Assembly Diagram.*

Figure 84. *Snowflakes.*

YARDAGE:

¼ yd. of muslin to impregnate with chemicals or kit that
comes with sufficient yardage for image-making

plus:

¼ yd. for sashing and inner border (⅜ yd. if binding is
to be included)

¼ yd. – outer borders

⅝ yd. – backing

CUT:

20 – 3½" squares of impregnated muslin

15 – 1" x 3½" sashing strips

4 – 1" x 14" sashing strips

2 – 1" x 15" inner border strips

2 – 1" x 19" inner border strips

2 – 2¼" x 20" outer border strips

2 – 2¼" x 23" outer border strips

1 – 21" x 24½" rectangle, backing

SNOWFLAKES
Color Plate XV

Dimensions: 19" x 22½"

Number of Pieces: 47

Construction Technique: Pieced.

Fabrics: Chemically prepared muslin, either from a kit or
prepared by yourself (see Resource List).

DIRECTIONS:

Transfer snowflake design to thin cardboard, such as
recipe card, file card, or oak tag. Carefully cut out using
small sharp scissors.

To produce the image, follow package or kit directions using the snowflake image you have made.

After squares have been laundered, dried, and
pressed, stitch short sashing strips to squares to form
rows, as in assembly diagram, *Fig. 85*. Attach the rows to
long sashings to form center of quilt. Add inner borders,
mitering corners. Do the same for the outer borders.

Quilting: Quilt around snowflake image and along all
seam lines. Using the quilting diagram provided, quilt
spinning stars into borders.

Complete quilt using Finishing Technique A or C.

Snowflake Design

84

Figure 85. *Assembly diagram.*

Quilting Template

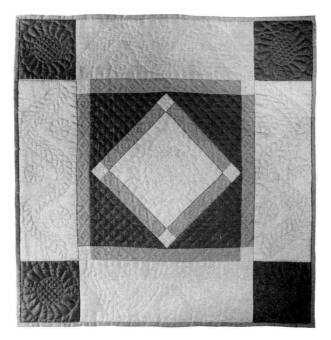

Figure 86. *Amish Diamond in a Square.*

YARDAGE:

⅜ yd. – A for center, small corner squares, and outside borders

¼ yd. – B for inside borders (or ⅜ yd. if including binding)

¼ yd. – C for large triangles and outside corners

½ yd. – backing

CUT:

1 – 5½" center square

4 – 1½" x 5½" small inner borders

8 – 1½" small corner squares

4 – large "X" triangles

4 – 1" x 10½" narrow outside borders

4 – 4½" x 12½" wide outside borders

4 – 4½" large corner squares

AMISH DIAMOND IN A SQUARE
Color Plate XVI

Dimensions: 20" x 20"
Number of Pieces: 29
Construction Technique: Pieced.
Fabrics: Bright solid colors with strong contrast.

DIRECTIONS:

Using the assembly diagram, *Fig. 87,* as a guide, stitch a narrow border to opposite sides of the center square. Add corner squares to each end of the remaining strips and attach as before. Next, attach triangles to all four sides of the unit you have just constructed, being careful not to stretch bias edges. Attach narrow outside borders and corners and finish quilt top by sewing on the wide outside borders and corners.

Quilting: Quilt top using patterns and diagrams provided. Complete quilt using Finishing Technique A or C.

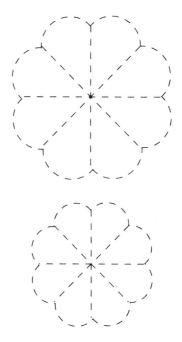

Quilting Templates

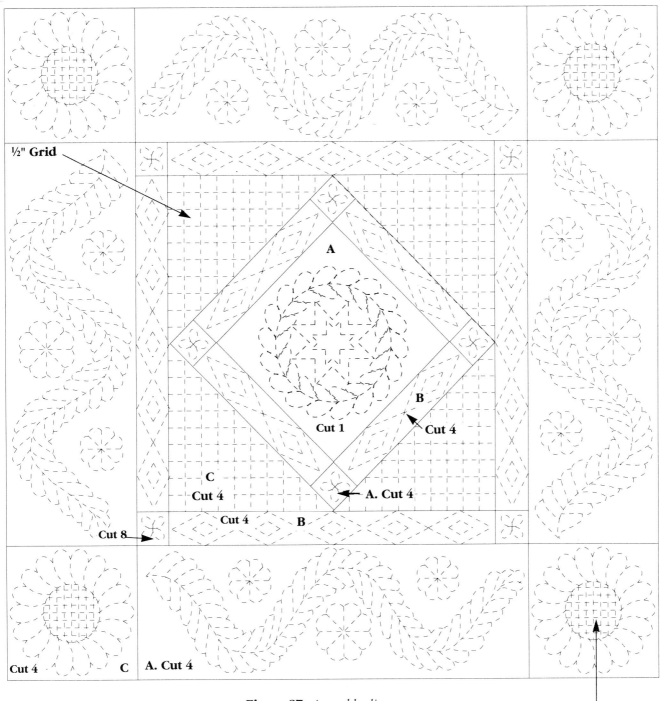

½" Grid

A

B

Cut 1

Cut 4

C
Cut 4

A. Cut 4

Cut 4

B

Cut 8

Cut 4   C

A. Cut 4

¼" Grid

Figure 87. *Assembly diagram.*

Quilting Patterns

**Amish Diamond in a
Square Patterns**

Quilting Patterns

Quilting Patterns

Amish Diamond in a Square Template

*Template Does Not Include
Seam Allowance.*

7"

5"

X

5"

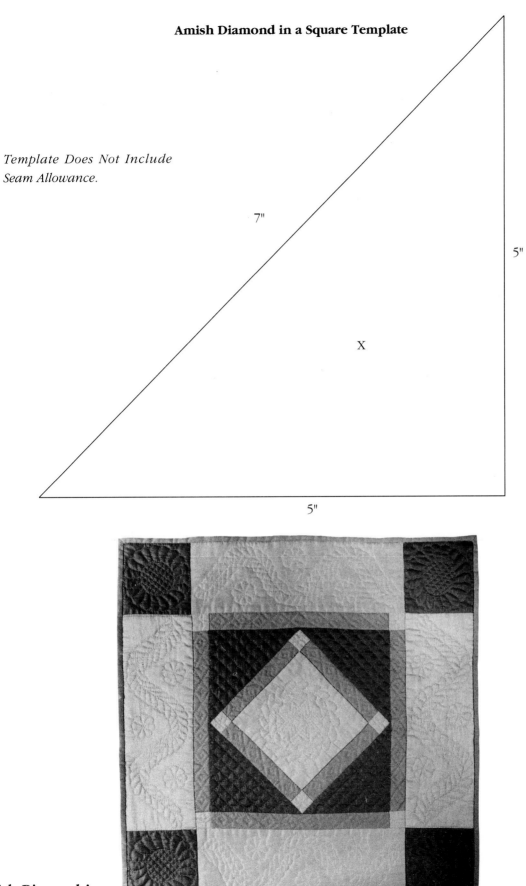

**Amish Diamond in
a Square**

Figure 88. *Joseph's Coat.*

YARDAGE:

⅝ yd. – R, red, backing and binding

¼ yd. – P, pink

¼ yd. – Y, yellow

¼ yd. – G, green

¼ yd. – B, blue

CUT:

(For center of quilt)

3 – 19½" x 1½" R strips

3 – 19½" x 1½" P strips

3 – 19½" x 1½" Y strips

3 – 19½" x 1½" G strips

3 – 19½" x 1½" B strips

(Borders)

4 – 18" x 1½" R strips

3 – 18" x 1½" P strips

3 – 18" x 1½" Y strips

3 – 18" x 1½" G strips

3 – 18" x 1½" B strips

(Corners)

4 – 1½" x 2¼" R strips

4 – 1½" x 2¼" P strips

1 – 20" x 24" backing

JOSEPH'S COAT
Color Plate XVII

Dimensions: 19" x 23"

Number of Pieces: 81

Construction Technique: Pieced.

Fabrics: Bright colors – solid cottons, polished cottons, cotton sateen, and chintz.

DIRECTIONS:

Center – Using assembly diagram, *Fig. 89*, stitch the 1½" x 19½" strips together in the following sequence: R + P + Y + G + B + R + P, etc. until the center of the quilt has been constructed.

Borders – Borders are assembled in the same sequence as the center of the quilt but in staggered rows, see *Fig. 90.* Assembly order is R + P + Y + G + B + R + P + Y + G + B + R + P + Y. Cut across these stitched rows on a 45° angle at a distance of 2¼" apart to make top and bottom border strips. Sew these strips in place.

For side borders begin at the Y end and add G + B + R. From this unit, cut two more ½" wide strips. Do not attach to quilt sides.

Corners – The corner squares are made by attaching one 1½" x 2½" R strip to one 1½" x 2½" P strip. Being careful not to stretch the bias edges, attach corner squares to side strips. Attach these rows to sides of quilt.

Quilting: Using the zigzag quilting pattern provided, quilt each center strip. Quilt along all seam lines. In borders, quilt along seam lines and down the middle of each stripe, see *Fig. 91.*

Complete quilt using Finishing Technique A or C.

Figure 89. *Assembly diagram.*

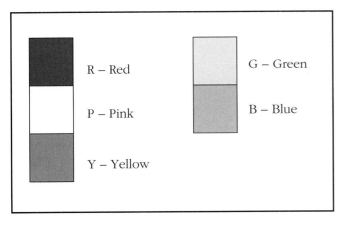

Assembly Key

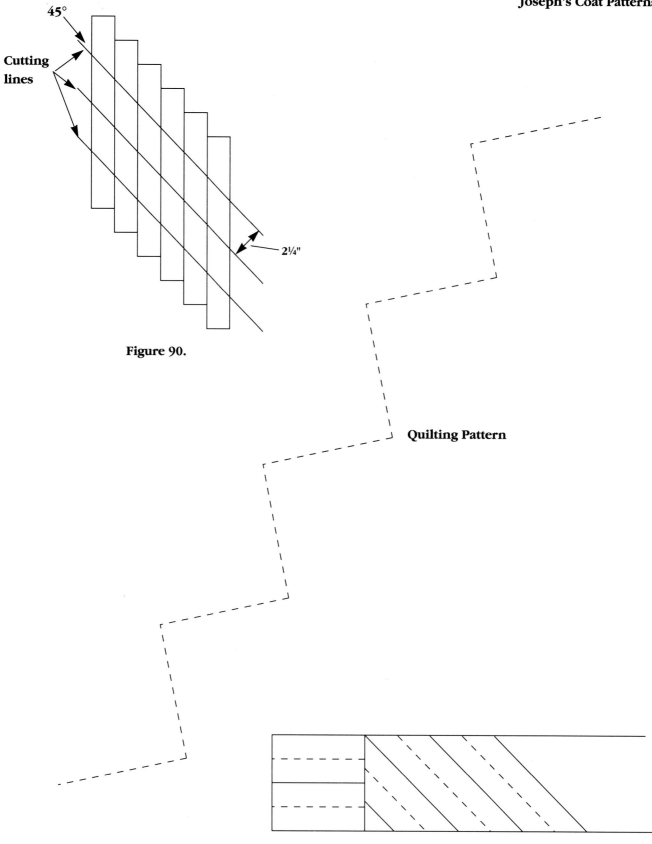

45°

Cutting
lines

2¼"

Figure 90.

Quilting Pattern

Figure 91.

Figure 92. *Zigzag.*

YARDAGE:

⅝ yd. – B, blue and backing and binding

¼ yd. – Y, yellow

¼ yd. – R, red

¼ yd. – P, pink

¼ yd. – G, green

(⅜ yd. of each if "quick-piecing" triangle squares)

CUT:

For triangles by the "quick-piecing" method:

(Center)

4 – 40" x 2" strips of B

4 – 40" x 2" strips of Y

4 – 40" x 2" strips of R

4 – 40" x 2" strips of P

4 – 40" x 2" strips of G

If using triangle template, cut:

52 – B

52 – Y

52 – R

52 – P

52 – G

ZIGZAG
Color Plate XVIII

Dimensions 19" x 23½"

Number of Pieces: 320

Construction Technique: Pieced.

Fabrics: Bright colors – solid cottons, polished cottons, and chintz.

DIRECTIONS:

Center – Using the directions for the "quick-piecing" technique in the General Instructions, seam two 2" x 40" strips of B to two 2" x 40" strips of Y. From these, cut 26 two-inch squares. Repeat this procedure for Y + R, R + P, P + G, and G + B. OR seam triangles together, B + Y, Y + R, R + P, P + G and G + B to form 2" squares.

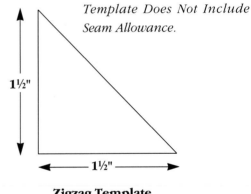

Template Does Not Include Seam Allowance.

1½"

1½"

Zigzag Template

PLUS:

For either method:

(Borders)

4 – 18" x 1½" strips of B

4 – 18" x 1½" strips of Y

4 – 18" x 1½" strips of R

4 – 18" x 1½" strips of P

4 – 18" x 1½" strips of G

1 – 20" x 24½" backing

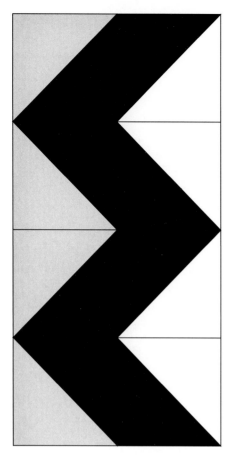

Figure 93.

Taking care not to stretch the bias edges, assemble squares into vertical rows, alternating the diagonal direction of each square, see *Fig. 93*. Seam rows together to form the quilt's center, as shown in *Fig. 94*.

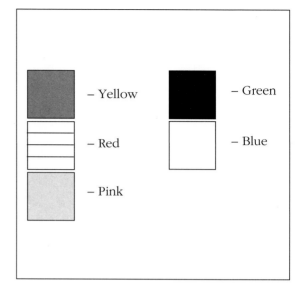

Assembly Key

Figure 94. *Assembly diagram.*

Borders – To make top and bottom borders, seam B + Y + R + P + G + B + Y + R + P + G + B + Y strips in a staggered fashion, as in *Fig. 95.*

Cut across to form two 2¼" wide rows. Continuing to stagger rows, add R + P + G + B + Y and cut two more 2¼" wide border strips.

Attach top and bottom border strips to center of quilt allowing each end to extend beyond the quilt for mitered corners, see *Fig. 96.* Add side borders, miter corners, and cut away excess seam allowances where necessary. OR construct border using the technique in the instructions for Joseph's Coat, page 92.

Quilting: Quilt along all seam lines and down the middle of each zigzag and outside border stripe.

Complete quilt using Finishing Technique C or A.

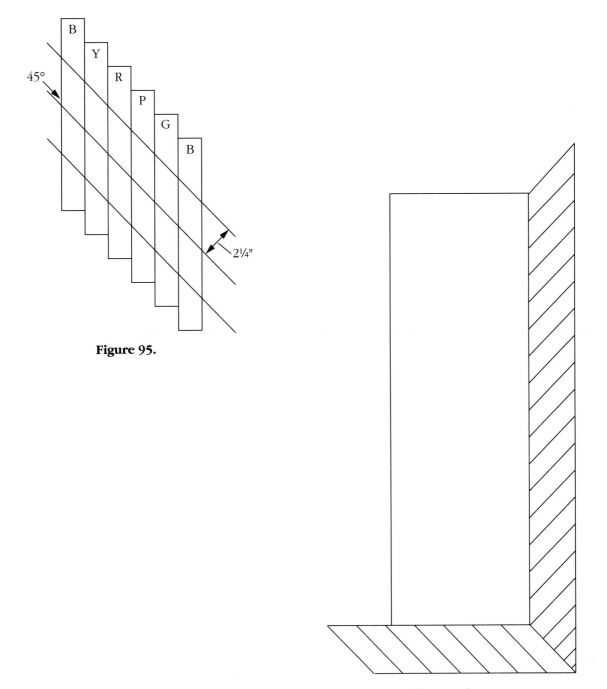

Figure 95.

Figure 96.

Figure 97. *Thistle Cradle Quilt.*

THISTLE CRADLE QUILT
Color Plate XIX

Dimensions: 17" x 23"

Number of Pieces: 121

Construction Techniques: Appliquéd, reverse and applied appliqué, and piecing.

Fabrics: Nineteenth-century reprints and unbleached muslin or tea-dyed cotton.

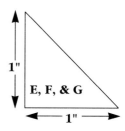

Templates Do Not Include Seam Allowance.

1" Square

Thistle Cradle Quilt Templates

YARDAGE:

scraps – center flower, top layer

scraps – center flower, under layer

¼ yd. – leaves, calyx, sawteeth

¼ yd. – thistle flowers, sawteeth, outer border

⅝ yd. – background, sawteeth, wide border

⅝ yd. – binding and backing

CUT:

1 – A (top flower)

1 – 1A (underlay)

3 – B

4 – C

3 – D

4 – H

1 – ½" x 7" strip from leaf fabric for stem

2 – 2½" x 22" strips for wide borders

2 – 2½" x 16" strips for wide borders

2 – 1¼" x 18" for outer borders

2 – 1¼" x 24" for outer borders

1 – 9½" x 15½" rectangle – background

PLUS:

24 – E

24 – F

48 – G

OR for "quick piecing"

2 – 1¼" x 26" strip of E

2 – 1¼" x 26" strip of F

1 – 1¼" x 20" strip of G

2 – 1¼" x width of cloth of G

98

DIRECTIONS:

Fold background rectangle in half both crosswise and lengthwise and press with iron. Open out and fold on the diagonals; press with iron. Be careful not to remove previous crease marks. Using these lines as your guide, lay out appliqué pieces and baste.

Appliqué pieces in place beginning with the four leaves, then the three thistle flowers, their calyxes, and the long stem. Stitch large flower over top of underlay fabric. Cut small slits for flower openings and reverse appliqué down.

Construct 48 triangles either by piecing 24 E's to G's and 24 F's to G's to form 1" squares (finished size) or by using the "quick piecing" technique. Assemble the finished squares into rows, alternating E and F squares; see assembly diagram, *Fig. 98*.

Add wide borders and miter corners. Do the same for the narrow outer borders.

Quilting: Quilt around all appliqué work and within the center flower, following the quilting lines on template. Fill the center background with grid quilting in parallel rows ¼" and ¾" apart; see photo, *Fig. 97*.

Quilt along seams in sawtooth border. Fill wide border with quilted version of large center flower and calyx using diagram provided. Quilt the outer border with elongated diamonds; using pattern provided.

Complete quilt using Finishing Technique A or C.

Figure 98. *Assembly diagram.*

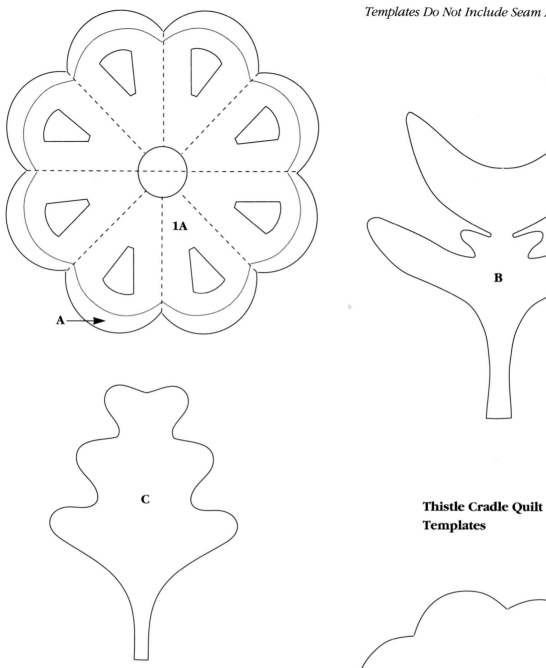

**Thistle Cradle Quilt
Templates**

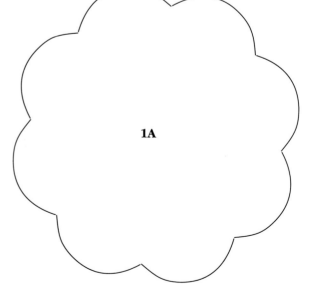

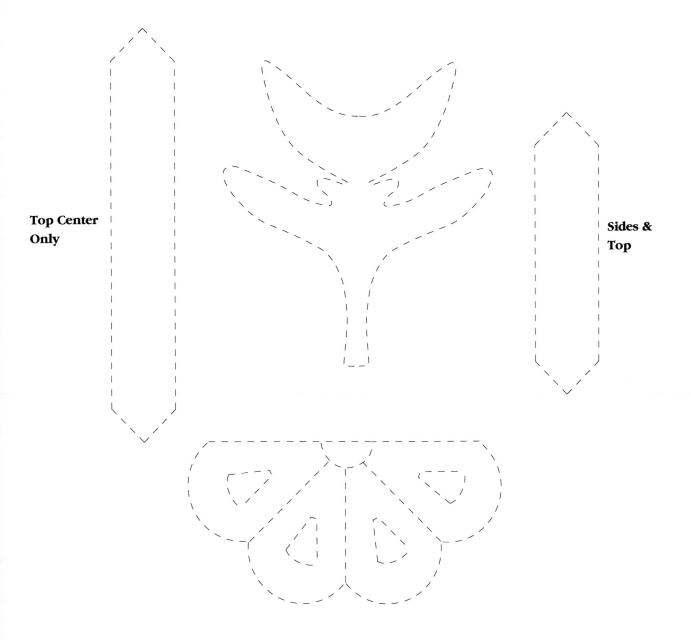

Top Center Only

Sides & Top

Quilting Patterns

RESOURCE LIST

BATTING

Fairfield Processing Corp.
P.O. Box 1130
Danbury, CT 06813
1-800-243-0989

Morning Glory Quilt Batting Products
Taylor Bedding Mfg. Co.
417 West 2nd
Taylor, TX 76574
1-800-234-9105
Mary Sharp
Director of Sales

Mountain Mist® Batting
The Stearns Technical Textile Co.
100 Williams Street
Cincinnati, Ohio 45215
1-800-345-7150

Warm Products (Cotton)
11232 120th N.E. #112
Kirkland, WA 98033
1-800-234-WARM

Packaged in a "cap" (Silk)
The Quilt Works, Inc.
Foothills Shopping Center
11117 Menaul, N.E.
Albuquerque, NM 87112
505-298-8210

Sold by the meter (Silk)
Sue Harris
The Mill
Tregoyd Mill
Three Cocks, Brecon
Powys LD3 OSW
Wales
Great Britain

Taos Mountain Wool Works (Wool)
P.O. Box 327
Arroyo Hondo, NM 87513
505-776-2925

BOOKS

The Art of Hand Appliqué, Laura Lee Fritz
Dyeing and Over-Dyeing of Cotton Fabrics, Judy M. Tescher
Fun and Fancy Machine Quiltmaking, Lois Smith
From Basics to Binding: A Complete Guide to Making Quilts,
Karen Kay Buckley
The Ins and Outs: Perfecting the Quilting Stitch, Patricia J. Morris
Marbling Fabrics for Quilts, Kathy Fawcett and Carol Shoaf
Quiltmaker's Guide: Basics & Beyond, Carol Doak
*Scarlet Ribbons, American Indian Technique for Today's
Quilters*, Helen Kelley
Stenciled Quilts for Christmas, Marie M. Sturmer

Available from AQS; call toll-free 1-800-626-5420
or write: AQS
         P.O. Box 3290
         Paducah, KY 42002-3290

COTTON SATEEN FABRICS

Cotton Patch
8250 E. 71st Street
Tulsa, OK 74133
918-252-1995

DYES

Pro Chemical & Dye Inc.
P.O. Box 14
Somerset, MA 02726
508-676-3838

FABRIC FADING POWDER

By Jupiter
6033 North 17th Avenue
Phoenix, AZ 85015
602-242-2574

QUILTING SUPPLIES

Cabin Fever Calicoes
P.O. Box 550106
Atlanta, GA 30355
1-800-762-2246
Catalog Available

Keepsake Quilting
Dover Street
P.O. Box 1459
Meredith, NH 03253 (catalog available)

HAND DYED FABRICS

Gail Garber Designs
P.O. Box 10028
Albuquerque, NM 87184
505-892-3354

New York Beauty Dye Works
604 N. Madison Street
Rome, N.Y. 13440
315-337-2363

Shades Inc.
2880 Holcomb Bridge Rd.
Suite B-9
Alpharetta, GA 30202
1-800-783-3933

MARBELIZED FABRICS

True Colors (also hand-dyed fabrics)
RD Box 91
Pittstown, NH 08867
908-735-7720 or 730-7398

Janet Wickell
Rt. 1 Box 44B
Brevard, NC 28712
704-884-7667

SUN-PRINT KITS, CHEMICALS, INSTRUCTIONS

Blueprints-Printables
1504 Industrial Way #7
Belmont, CA 94002

Grandma's Graphics, Inc.
20 Birling Gap
Fairport, N.Y. 14450-3916

TEMPLATE PLASTIC WITH GRIDS

LAM-I-GRAPHS
Extra Special Products
Box 777
Greenville, Ohio 45331

TEMPLATE-GRAPH
Quilter's Rule
3201 Davie Blvd.
Ft. Lauderdale, FL 33312

ORVUS® SOAP

Talas
213 W. 35th St.
New York, NY 10001
212-736-7744

BIBLIOGRAPHY

Association of Community Arts Councils of Kansas. *Kansas Quilts — An Exhibition of Antique and Contemporary Quilts from Kansas Collections.*

Bishop, Robert. *New Discoveries in American Quilts.* E.P. Dutton Co., Inc., New York, 1975.

Bishop, Robert and Elizabeth Safanda. *A Gallery of Amish Quilts.* E.P. Dutton Co., Inc., New York, 1976.

Bishop, Robert, William Secord, Judith Reiter Weismann. *Quilts, Coverlets, Rugs, and Samplers, The Knopf Collector's Guide.* Alfred A. Knopf, New York, 1982.

Blum, Dilys, Jack L. Lindsey. *19th-Century Appliqué Quilts.* Philadelphia Museum of Art Bulletin, Philadelphia, PA., 1989.

Brackman, Barbara. *Clues in the Calico.* EPM Publishers Inc., 1989.

Ferrero, Pat, Elaine Hedges, Julie Silber. *Hearts and Hands: The Influence of Women and Quilts on American Society.* Quilt Digest Press, San Francisco, CA, 1987.

Finley, Ruth E. *Old Patchwork Quilts and the Women Who Made Them.* Charles T. Branford Co., Newton Centre, MA, 1957.

Fox, Sandi; curator. *19th Century American Patchwork Quilt.* The Seibu Museum Art Catalogue, Japan, 1983.

Haders, Phyllis. *The Warner Collector's Guide to American Quilts.* Main Street Press Division of Warner Books Inc., New York, 1981.

Hall, Carrie A. and Rose G. Kretsinger. *The Romance of the Patchwork Quilt.* Caxton Printers Ltd., Caldwell, ID, 1935.

Hoffman, Victoria. *Quilts, A Window to the Past.* Museum of American Textile History, Andover, MA, 1991.

Hoke, Donald; editor. *Dressing The Bed.* Catalogue of the Milwaukee Public Museum. Milwaukee, WI, 1985.

Holstein, Jonathan. *The Pieced Quilt.* New York Graphics Society, Boston, 1973.

Houck, Carter and Myron Miller. *American Quilts and How to Make Them.* Charles Scribner's Sons, New York, 1975.

Hughes, Trudie. *Template Free Quiltmaking.* That Patchwork Place, Bothell, WA, 1986.

Johnson, Bruce. *A Child's Comfort.* Harcourt, Brace, & Jovanovich in association with the Museum of Folk Art, New York, 1977.

Katzenberg, Dena S. *Baltimore Album Quilts.* Baltimore Museum of Art, 1981.

Khin, Yvonne M. *The Collector's Dictionary of Quilt Names and Patterns.* Acropolis Books Ltd., Washington, D.C., 1980.

Kiracofe and Kile. *The Quilt Digest.* Kiracofe and Kile, San Francisco, 1986.

Lasansky, Jeanette. *In the Heart of Pennsylvania. 19th & 20th Century Quiltmaking Traditions.* The Oral Traditions Project of Union County Historical Society, Leesburg, PA, 1985.

Pieced By Mother. Over 100 Years of Quiltmaking Traditions. The Oral Traditions Project of Union County Historical Society, Lewisburg, PA, 1987.

Leone, Diana. *Fine Hand Quilting.* Leone Publications, Los Altos, CA, 1986.

Martin, Nancy. *Pieces of the Past.* That Patchwork Place, Inc., Bothell, WA, 1986.

Nelson, Cyril I. and Carter Houck. *The Treasury of American Quilts.* E.P. Dutton Co., Inc., New York, 1982.

Nicholas, Marion. *Encyclopedia of Embroidery Stitches, Including Crewel.* Dover Publications Inc., New York, 1974.

Orlofsky, Patsy and Myron. *Quilts in America.* McGraw-Hill Book Co., New York, 1974.

Pfeffer, Susan. *Quilt Masterpieces.* Hugh Lauter, Levin Ass., Inc., New York, 1988.

Safford, Caleton L. and Robert Bishop. *America's Quilts and Coverlets.* E.P. Dutton Co., Inc., New York, 1980.

Weissman, Judith R. and Wendy Lavitt. *Labors of Love.* Alfred A. Knopf, New York, 1987.

Wiss, Audrey and Doublass. *Folk Quilts and How to Recreate Them.* Main St. Press, Pittstown, NJ, 1983.

∾American Quilter's Society∾

dedicated to publishing books for today's quilters

The following AQS publications are currently available:

- **Adapting Architectural Details for Quilts,** Carol Wagner, #2282: AQS, 1991, 88 pages, softbound, $12.95
- **American Beauties: Rose & Tulip Quilts,** Gwen Marston & Joe Cunningham, #1907: AQS, 1988, 96 pages, softbound, $14.95
- **America's Pictorial Quilts,** Caron L. Mosey, #1662: AQS, 1985, 112 pages, hardbound, $19.95
- **Applique Designs: My Mother Taught Me to Sew,** Faye Anderson, #2121: AQS, 1990, 80 pages, softbound, $12.95
- **Arkansas Quilts: Arkansas Warmth,** Arkansas Quilter's Guild, Inc., #1908: AQS, 1987, 144 pages, hardbound, $24.95
- **The Art of Hand Applique,** Laura Lee Fritz, #2122: AQS, 1990, 80 pages, softbound, $14.95
- **...Ask Helen More About Quilting Designs,** Helen Squire, #2099: AQS, 1990, 54 pages, 17 x 11, spiral-bound, $14.95
- **Award-Winning Quilts & Their Makers: Vol. I, The Best of AQS Shows – 1985-1987,** #2207: AQS, 1991, 232 pages, softbound, $24.95
- **Award-Winning Quilts & Their Makers: Vol. II, The Best of AQS Shows – 1988-1989,** #2354: AQS, 1992, 176 pages, softbound, $24.95
- **Award-Winning Quilts & Their Makers: Vol. III, The Best of AQS Shows – 1990-1991,** #3425: AQS, 1993, 180 pages, softbound, $24.95
- **Classic Basket Quilts,** Elizabeth Porter & Marianne Fons, #2208: AQS, 1991, 128 pages, softbound, $16.95
- **A Collection of Favorite Quilts,** Judy Florence, #2119: AQS, 1990, 136 pages, softbound, $18.95
- **Creative Machine Art,** Sharee Dawn Roberts, #2355: AQS, 1992, 142 pages, 9 x 9, softbound, $24.95
- **Dear Helen, Can You Tell Me?...all about quilting designs,** Helen Squire, #1820: AQS, 1987, 51 pages, 17 x 11, spiral-bound, $12.95
- **Dye Painting!,** Ann Johnston, #3399: AQS, 1992, 88 pages, softbound, $19.95
- **Dyeing & Overdyeing of Cotton Fabrics,** Judy Mercer Tescher, #2030: AQS, 1990, 54 pages, softbound, $9.95
- **Flavor Quilts for Kids to Make: Complete Instructions for Teaching Children to Dye, Decorate & Sew Quilts,** Jennifer Amor #2356: AQS, 1991, 120 pages, softbound, $12.95
- **From Basics to Binding: A Complete Guide to Making Quilts,** Karen Kay Buckley, #2381: AQS, 1992, 160 pages, softbound, $16.95
- **Fun & Fancy Machine Quiltmaking,** Lois Smith, #1982: AQS, 1989, 144 pages, softbound, $19.95
- **Gallery of American Quilts 1830-1991: Book III,** #3421: AQS, 1992, 128 pages, softbound, $19.95
- **The Grand Finale: A Quilter's Guide to Finishing Projects,** Linda Denner, #1924: AQS, 1988, 96 pages, softbound, $14.95
- **Heirloom Miniatures,** Tina M. Gravatt, #2097: AQS, 1990, 64 pages, softbound, $9.95
- **Infinite Stars,** Gayle Bong, #2283: AQS, 1992, 72 pages, softbound, $12.95
- **The Ins and Outs: Perfecting the Quilting Stitch,** Patricia J. Morris, #2120: AQS, 1990, 96 pages, softbound, $9.95
- **Irish Chain Quilts: A Workbook of Irish Chains & Related Patterns,** Joyce B. Peaden, #1906: AQS, 1988, 96 pages, softbound, $14.95
- **The Log Cabin Returns to Kentucky: Quilts from the Pilgrim/Roy Collection,** Gerald Roy and Paul Pilgrim, #3329: AQS, 1992, 36 pages, 9 x 7, softbound, $12.95
- **Marbling Fabrics for Quilts: A Guide for Learning & Teaching,** Kathy Fawcett & Carol Shoaf, #2206: AQS, 1991, 72 pages, softbound, $12.95
- **More Projects and Patterns: A Second Collection of Favorite Quilts,** Judy Florence, #3330: AQS, 1992, 152 pages, softbound, $18.95
- **Nancy Crow: Quilts and Influences,** Nancy Crow, #1981: AQS, 1990, 256 pages, 9 x 12, hardcover, $29.95
- **Nancy Crow: Work in Transition,** Nancy Crow, #3331: AQS, 1992, 32 pages, 9 x 10, softbound, $12.95
- **New Jersey Quilts – 1777 to 1950: Contributions to an American Tradition,** The Heritage Quilt Project of New Jersey; text by Rachel Cochran, Rita Erickson, Natalie Hart & Barbara Schaffer, #3332: AQS, 1992, 256 pages, softbound, $29.95
- **No Dragons on My Quilt,** Jean Ray Laury with Ritva Laury & Lizabeth Laury, #2153: AQS, 1990, 52 pages, hardcover, $12.95
- **Oklahoma Heritage Quilts,** Oklahoma Quilt Heritage Project #2032: AQS, 1990, 144 pages, softbound, $19.95
- **Old Favorites in Miniature,** Tina Gravatt, #3469: AQS, 1993, 104 pages, softbound, $15.95
- **Quilt Groups Today: Who They Are, Where They Meet, What They Do, and How to Contact Them; A Complete Guide for 1992-1993,** #3308: AQS, 1992, 336 pages, softbound, $14.95
- **Quilting Patterns from Native American Designs,** Dr. Joyce Mori, #3467: AQS, 1993, 80 pages, softbound, $12.95
- **Quilting with Style: Principles for Great Pattern Design,** Gwen Marston & Joe Cunningham, #3470: AQS, 1993, 192 pages, 9 x 12, hardcover, $24.95
- **Quiltmaker's Guide: Basics & Beyond,** Carol Doak, #2284: AQS, 1992, 208 pages, softbound, $19.95
- **Quilts: Old & New, A Similar View,** Paul D. Pilgrim and Gerald E. Roy, #3715: AQS, 1993, 40 pages, softbound, $12.95
- **Quilts: The Permanent Collection – MAQS,** #2257: AQS, 1991, 100 pages, 10 x 6½, softbound, $9.95
- **Sensational Scrap Quilts,** Darra Duffy Williamson, #2357: AQS, 1992, 152 pages, softbound, $24.95
- **Show Me Helen...How to Use Quilting Designs,** Helen Squire, #3375: AQS, 1993, 155 pages, softbound, $15.95
- **Sets & Borders,** Gwen Marston & Joe Cunningham, #1821: AQS, 1987, 104 pages, softbound, $14.95
- **Somewhere in Between: Quilts and Quilters of Illinois,** Rita Barrow Barber, #1790: AQS, 1986, 78 pages, softbound, $14.95
- **Stenciled Quilts for Christmas,** Marie Monteith Sturmer, #2098: AQS, 1990, 104 pages, softbound, $14.95
- **A Treasury of Quilting Designs,** Linda Goodmon Emery, #2029: AQS, 1990, 80 pages, 14 x 11, spiral-bound, $14.95
- **Wonderful Wearables: A Celebration of Creative Clothing,** Virginia Avery, #2286: AQS, 1991, 184 pages, softbound, $24.95

These books can be found in local bookstores and quilt shops. If you are unable to locate a title in your area, you can order by mail from AQS, P.O. Box 3290, Paducah, KY 42002-3290. Please add $1 for the first book and 40¢ for each additional one to cover postage and handling. (International orders please add $1.50 for the first book and $1 for each additional one.)